Views and Values

Diverse Readings on Universal Themes

Kari Sayers
Marymount College

THOMSON

HEINLE

Australia Canada Mexico Singapore Spain United Kingdom United States

THOMSON

™

HEINLE

Views and Values, Second Edition
Diverse Readings on Universal Themes
Kari Sayers

Publisher: Earl McPeek
Acquisitions Editor: Stephen Dalphin
Developmental Editor: Jill Johnson
Market Strategist: John Myers
Project Manager: Barrett Lackey

Cover/Chapter Opening credit: Eyewire/Rubberball Productions

Printed in the United States of America
4 5 6 7 8 9 10   06 05 04 03 02

For more information contact Heinle, 25 Thomson Place, Boston, MA 02210 USA,
or you can visit our Internet site at http://www.heinle.com

ISBN: 0-15-506354-5

Library of Congress Catalog Card Number:
        00-104422

Thematic Contents

Myths and Tales   165

Race, Culture, and Identity   199

Contents by Country

To the Instructor

Since the first edition of *Views and Values* appeared in 1996, more basic reading and writing instructors seem to agree that students need to be exposed to a variety of reading material; not only short essays, but also longer pieces with more depth.

This edition continues to provide excellent literary selections from our classical heritage, both fiction and nonfiction that require some scrutiny and analysis. Because of some teachers' recommendations, we have replaced a couple of the least popular stories with two myths and a tale. We have also added more topics for writing and further discussion that require comparison and contrast of two or more reading selections.

As before, the objective of this book is to develop not only reading and writing skills, but also the ability to think critically. Students will be exposed to excellent literature by prize-winning authors from around the world, beautifully written short fiction and nonfiction with real depth, stories that make students feel and experience events with well-drawn characters, and stories that invite students to think about important values in their own daily lives.

Yet, even though the stories have been chosen for their high literary quality, they have also been chosen for their relative brevity and accessibility. Whether old or new, all the stories make simple statements about the human condition that today's students can easily understand and relate to.

Apparatus

Preceding each story are a few broad, open-ended questions that are meant to motivate the students to read and to create a "hook" for the students to hang the story on. Instructors may, of course, pose more questions of their own. A simple glossary also precedes most stories.

Following each story are comprehension and discussion questions. The questions are not separated into independent skills because it has been our experience that reading skills cannot always be neatly divided into separate categories. Nevertheless, instructors will recognize such skills as focusing on important details that make up the main point; making inferences; drawing conclusions; sequencing; detecting an author's bias and tone as well as a story's mood; appreciating style; evaluating evidence; and making judgments. However, the questions have been grouped into broader categories such as recalling, interpreting, and evaluating. Many poor readers lack the ability to visualize what they read. By constantly asking them to focus on description and plot details, this important skill will improve. Similarly, by repeated practice with questions that require interpreting and evaluating, students develop critical thinking skills that will carry over to reading other types of prose as well as to their own writing. Some instructors may prefer to assign only these more open-ended questions.

Also following each story are several writing topics either based on the story itself or related to a theme in the story. Some topics lend themselves to paragraph practice, whereas other topics are broader and may be better developed in essays as indicated. Suggested thesis statements are included as a starting point for discussion and writing, but are not meant to preclude other ways of developing a particular topic.

An instructor's manual with possible answers to the comprehension questions is available. Included in the instructor's manual is also a suggestion for a different way to group the stories other than by thematic content, multiple-choice questions and true/false quick-check tests, as well as sample paragraphs and essays written by students in response to the writing topics. Although this reader is intended as a supplement to a core reading skills or writing textbook, we have included a summary of the most frequently taught reading strategies and the most common points of the writing process for those who choose to teach without a core text.

Finally, the reading level of each story has been measured using the Fry method and recorded in the manual.

To the Student

If you want to improve your reading and writing skills, this book is for you. Of course, being a college student you probably think you read and write fairly well, but may lack some vocabulary and grammar skills for advanced work. While having good vocabulary and grammar skills is essential to both reading and writing, equally important is clear thinking. In addition to developing your vocabulary and sentence structure, this book, then, will develop your ability to think clearly and critically about what you have read so that you can get ready to write. While practicing your reading and writing skills you will also meet characters from different places and backgrounds, experience their problems and pleasures, and learn from their mistakes. Welcome to the wonderful world of literature!

Before you start reading, take a moment to reflect on the questions preceding each story and look over the vocabulary. Then read the story carefully, preferably in one sitting, and answer the comprehension questions after the story. Finally, try to relate the events in the stories to your own life by focusing on the topics for writing and further discussion.

To familiarize yourself with this book, look at the Contents How are the stories arranged in the Contents? What are some of the general themes the stories explore? How do these themes relate to you?

Although some stories are new, many have also been around for a long time and are part of our classical heritage. However, whether contemporary or classical, all the stories have been chosen for their appeal to college students of all ages and from all walks of life. Happy reading!

Acknowledgments

I wish to thank my colleagues and students at Marymount College for their criticism and ideas. Special thanks to Ottillie Boboc, Charlene Butwell, Joan Cashion, Mary Beth Culp, Jennifer Kasinskas, Belle Levinson-Brubaker, Greg Levonian, Al Lewis, Ruth Proctor, Nancy Sanders, Bruce Schwartz, Eileen Smith, Jean Smith, Charles Spurgeon, and Rhonda Wiley.

Furthermore, I wish to extend my appreciation to the many reviewers for their excellent recommendations and suggestions: Peggy Harbors, Nashville State Tech; Mark Medvetz, University of Montana at Missoula; Geraldine Daugherty, University of Southern Colorado; Marilyn Kay Trentham, DeKalb Technical Institute; Karen O'Donnell, Finger Lakes Community College; Suzanne Crawford, Saddleback College.

I am also grateful to Jill Johnson and Steve Dalphin along with the editors and assistants at Harcourt for their professional yet friendly approach to publishing. I would also like to thank Vickie Lanius and the staff at Progressive Publishing Alternatives for their helpful assistance.

Finally, I want to thank my husband for his endless patience, support, and love.

Children and Adults

Innocence and Experience

A Mother in Mannville

Marjorie Rawlings

About the Author

Marjorie Rawlings was an American novelist and short story writer who spent most of her adult life in Florida. Her best-known novel, *The Yearling*, was awarded a Pulitzer Prize and made into a popular movie in 1946, starring Gregory Peck and Jane Wyman. Marjorie Rawlings died in 1953.

 ### Something to Think About

How does our imagination help us cope with reality? What is perhaps an orphan's greatest wish?

 ### Words to Keep in Mind

(The numbers in parentheses refer to the paragraphs in which the words first appear.)

rhododendron *(3)* shrub with pink, white, or purple flowers

hemlocks *(3)* poisonous plant with small white flowers

malaria *(5)* (literally, "bad air") disease transmitted by mosquitoes

corn shocks *(5)* stalks of corn stacked together to dry

mangled *(12)* mutilated, crippled

stoop *(14)* porch or step in front of a house

asters *(14)* plant with purplish flowers that bloom in fall

suffused *(20)* spread throughout

kindling *(23)* small pieces of dry wood used to start a fire

subterfuge *(28)* plan to hide the truth

treacherously *(32)* dangerously

impelled *(45)* driven

parturition *(49)* childbirth

thistledown *(71)* white, fluffy down formed on thistle, a weed with prickly leaves and stems and purple flowers

trifle *(73)* a little

abstracted *(73)* absent-minded

anomalous *(73)* abnormal

ecstasy *(74)* extreme happiness

vermilion *(74)* bright red

T he orphanage is high in the Carolina mountains. Some- 1
times in winter the snowdrifts are so deep that the insti-
tution is cut off from the village below, from all the world. Fog
hides the mountain peaks, the snow swirls down the valleys,
and a wind blows so bitterly that the orphanage boys who take
the milk twice daily to the baby cottage reach the door with fingers stiff in an agony of numbness.

"Or when we carry trays from the cookhouse for the ones 2
that are sick," Jerry said, "we get our faces frostbit, because we
can't put our hands over them. I have gloves," he added. "Some
of the boys don't have any."

He liked the late spring, he said. The rhododendron was in 3
bloom, a carpet of color, across the mountainsides, soft as the
May winds that stirred the hemlocks. He called it laurel.

"It's pretty when the laurel blooms," he said. "Some of it's 4
pink and some of it's white."

I was there in the autumn. I wanted quiet, isolation, to do 5
some troublesome writing. I wanted mountain air to blow out
the malaria from too long a time in the subtropics. I was home-
sick, too, for the flaming of maples in October, and for corn
shocks and pumpkins and black walnut trees and the lift of hills.
I found them all, living in a cabin that belonged to the orphanage, half a mile beyond the orphanage farm. When I took the
cabin, I asked for a boy or man to come and chop wood for the
fireplace. The first few days were warm, I found what wood I
needed about the cabin, no one came, and I forgot the order.

I looked up from my typewriter one late afternoon, a little 6
startled. A boy stood at the door, and my pointer dog, my companion, was at his side and had not barked to warn me. The boy
was probably twelve years old, but undersized. He wore overalls and a torn shirt, and was barefooted.

He said, "I can chop some wood today." 7

I said, "But I have a boy coming from the orphanage." 8

"I'm the boy." 9

"You? But you're small." 10

"Size don't matter, chopping wood," he said. "Some of the 11
big boys don't chop good. I've been chopping wood at the
orphanage a long time."

I visualized mangled and inadequate branches for my fires. I 12
was well into my work and not inclined to conversation. I was a
little blunt.

"Very well. There's the ax. Go ahead and see what you can 13
do."

I went back to work, closing the door. At first the sound of 14
the boy dragging brush annoyed me. Then he began to chop.
The blows were rhythmic and steady, and shortly I had forgotten
him, the sound no more of an interruption than a consistent rain.
I suppose an hour and a half passed, for when I stopped and
stretched, and heard the boy's steps on the cabin stoop, the sun
was dropping behind the farthest mountain, and the valleys
were purple with something deeper than the asters.

The boy said, "I have to go to supper now. I can come again 15
tomorrow evening."

I said, "I'll pay you now for what you've done," thinking I   16
should probably have to insist on an older boy. "Ten cents an
hour?"

"Anything is all right."   17

We went together back of the cabin. An astonishing amount   18
of solid wood had been cut. There were cherry logs and heavy
roots of rhododendron, and blocks from the waste pine and oak
left from the building of the cabin.

"But you've done as much as a man," I said, "This is a splen-   19
did pile."

I looked at him, actually, for the first time. His hair was the   20
color of the corn shocks and his eyes, very direct, were like the
mountain sky when rain is pending—gray, with a shadowing of
that miraculous blue. As I spoke, a light came over him, as
though the setting sun had touched him with the same suffused
glory with which it touched the mountains. I gave him a quarter.

"You may come tomorrow," I said, "and thank you very   21
much."

He looked at me, and at the coin, and seemed to want to   22
speak, but could not, and turned away.

"I'll split kindling tomorrow," he said over his thin ragged   23
shoulder. "You'll need kindling and medium wood and logs and
backlogs."

At daylight I was half wakened by the sound of chopping.   24
Again it was so even in texture that I went back to sleep. When I
left my bed in the cool morning, the boy had come and gone,
and a stack of kindling was neat against the cabin wall. He came
again after school in the afternoon and worked until time to
return to the orphanage. His name was Jerry; he was twelve
years old, and he had been at the orphanage since he was four. I
could picture him at four, with the same grave gray-blue eyes
and the same—independence? No, the word that comes to me is
"integrity."

The word means something very special to me, and the qual-   25
ity for which I use it is a rare one. My father had it—there is
another of whom I am almost sure—but almost no man of my
acquaintance possesses it with the clarity, the purity, the simplic-

ity of a mountain stream. But the boy Jerry had it. It is bedded on courage, but it is more than brave. It is honest, but it is more than honesty. The ax handle broke one day. Jerry said the woodshop at the orphanage would repair it. I brought money to pay for the job and he refused it.

"I'll pay for it," he said. "I broke it. I brought the ax down careless." 26

"But no one hits accurately every time," I told him. "The fault was in the wood of the handle. I'll see the man from whom I bought it." 27

It was only then that he would take the money. He was standing back of his own carelessness. He was a free-will agent and he chose to do careful work, and if he failed, he took the responsibility without subterfuge. 28

And he did for me the unnecessary thing, the gracious thing, that we find done only by the great of heart. Things no training can teach, for they are done on the instant, with no predicated experience. He found a cubbyhole beside the fireplace that I had not noticed. There, of his own accord, he put kindling and "medium" wood, so that I might always have dry fire material ready in case of sudden wet weather. A stone was loose in the rough walk to the cabin. He dug a deeper hole and steadied it, although he came, himself, by a short cut over the bank. I found that when I tried to return his thoughtfulness with such things as candy and apples, he was wordless. "Thank you" was, perhaps, an expression for which he had had no use, for his courtesy was instinctive. He only looked at the gift and at me, and a curtain lifted, so that I saw deep into the clear well of his eyes, and gratitude was there, and affection, soft over the firm granite of his character. 29

He made simple excuses to come and sit with me. I could no more have turned him away than if he had been physically hungry. I suggested once that the best time for us to visit was just before supper, when I left off my writing. After that, he waited always until my typewriter had been some time quiet. One day I worked until nearly dark. I went outside the cabin, having forgotten him. I saw him going up over the hill in the twilight 30 toward the orphanage. When I sat down on my stoop, a place was warm from his body where he had been sitting.

He became intimate, of course, with my pointer, Pat. There is 31 a strange communion between a boy and a dog. Perhaps they possess the same singleness of spirit, the same kind of wisdom. It is difficult to explain, but it exists. When I went across the state for a week end, I left the dog in Jerry's charge. I gave him the dog whistle and the key to the cabin, and left sufficient food. He was to come two or three times a day and let out the dog, and feed and exercise him. I should return Sunday night, and Jerry would take out the dog for the last time Sunday afternoon and then leave the key under an agreed hiding place.

My return was belated and fog filled the mountain passes so 32 treacherously that I dared not drive at night. The fog held the next morning, and it was Monday noon before I reached the cabin. The dog had been fed and cared for that morning. Jerry came early in the afternoon, anxious.

"The superintendent said nobody would drive in the fog," 33 he said. "I came just before bedtime last night and you hadn't come. So I brought Pat some of my breakfast this morning. I wouldn't have let anything happen to him."

"I was sure of that. I didn't worry." 34

"When I heard about the fog, I thought you'd know." 35

He was needed for work at the orphanage and he had to 36 return at once. I gave him a dollar in payment, and he looked at it and went away. But that night he came in the darkness and knocked at the door.

"Come in, Jerry," I said, "if you're allowed to be away this 37 late."

"I told maybe a story," he said. "I told them I thought you 38 would want to see me."

"That's true," I assured him, and I saw his relief. "I want to 39 hear about how you managed with the dog."

He sat by the fire with me, with no other light, and told me of 40 their two days together. The dog lay close to him, and found a comfort there that I did not have for him. And it seemed to me that being with my dog, and caring for him, had brought the boy and me, too, together, so that he felt that he belonged to me as well as to the animal.

"He stayed right with me," he told me, "except when he ran 11 in the laurel. He likes the laurel. I took him up over the hill and we both ran fast. There was a place where the grass was high and I lay down in it and hid. I could hear Pat hunting for me. He found my trail and he barked. When he found me, he acted crazy, and he ran around and around me, in circles."

We watched the flames. 42

"That's an apple log," he said. "It burns the prettiest of any 43 wood."

We were very close. 44

He was suddenly impelled to speak of things he had not 45 spoken of before, nor had I cared to ask him.

"You look a little bit like my mother," he said. "Especially in 46 the dark, by the fire."

"But you were only four, Jerry, when you came here. You 47 have remembered how she looked, all these years?"

"My mother lives in Mannville," he said. 48

For a moment, finding that he had a mother shocked me as 49 greatly as anything in my life has ever done, and I did not know why it disturbed me. Then I understood my distress. I was filled with a passionate resentment that any woman should go away and leave her son. A fresh anger added itself. A son like this one— The orphanage was a wholesome place, the executives were kind, good people, the food was more than adequate, the boys were healthy, a ragged shirt was no hardship, nor the doing of clean labor. Granted, perhaps, that the boy felt no lack, what blood fed the bowels of a woman who did not yearn over this child's lean body that had come in parturition out of her own? At four he would have looked the same as now. Nothing, I thought, nothing in life could change those eyes. His quality must be apparent to an idiot, a fool. I burned with questions I could not ask. In any, I was afraid, there would be pain.

"Have you seen her, Jerry—lately?" 50

"I see her every summer. She sends for me." 51

I wanted to cry out, "Why are you not with her? How can   52
she let you go away again?"

He said, "She comes up here from Mannville whenever she   53
can. She doesn't have a job now."

His face shone in the firelight.   54

"She wanted to give me a puppy, but they can't let any one   55
boy keep a puppy. You remember the suit I had on last Sunday?"
He was plainly proud. "She sent me that for Christmas. The
Christmas before that"—he drew a long breath, savoring the
memory—"she sent me a pair of skates."

"Roller skates?"   56

My mind was busy, making pictures of her, trying to under-   57
stand her. She had not, then, entirely deserted or forgotten him.
But why, then— I thought, "I must not condemn her without
knowing."

"Roller skates. I let the other boys use them. They're always   58
borrowing them. But they're careful of them."

What circumstance other than poverty—   59

"I'm going to take the dollar you gave me for taking care of   60
Pat," he said, "and buy her a pair of gloves."

I could only say, "That will be nice. Do you know her size?"   61

"I think it's 8½," he said.   62

He looked at my hands.   63

"Do you wear 8½?" he asked.   64

"No. I wear a smaller size, a 6."   65

"Oh! Then I guess her hands are bigger than yours."   66

I hated her. Poverty or no, there was other food than bread,   67
and the soul could starve as quickly as the body. He was taking
his dollar to buy gloves for her big stupid hands, and she lived
away from him, in Mannville, and contented herself with sending him skates.

"She likes white gloves," he said. "Do you think I can get   68
them for a dollar?"

"I think so," I said.   69

I decided that I should not leave the mountains without   70
seeing her and knowing for myself why she had done this
thing.

The human mind scatters its interests as though made of 71
thistledown, and every wind stirs and moves it. I finished my
work. It did not please me, and I gave my thoughts to another
field. I should need some Mexican material.

I made arrangements to close my Florida place Mexico 72
immediately, and doing the writing there, if conditions were
favorable. Then, Alaska with my brother. After that, heaven
knew what or where.

I did not take time to go to Mannville to see Jerry's mother, 73
nor even to talk with the orphanage officials about her. I was a
trifle abstracted about the boy, because of my work and plans.
And after my first fury at her—we did not speak of her again—
his having a mother, any sort at all, not far away, in Mannville,
relieved me of the ache I had had about him. He did not question the anomalous relation. He was not lonely. It was none of
my concern.

He came every day and cut my wood and did small helpful 74
favors and stayed to talk. The days had become cold, and often I
let him come inside the cabin. He would lie on the floor in front
of the fire, with one arm across the pointer, and they would both
doze and wait quietly for me. Other days they ran with a common ecstasy through the laurel, and since the asters were now
gone, he brought me back vermilion maple leaves, and chestnut
boughs dripping with imperial yellow. I was ready to go.

I said to him, "You have been my good friend, Jerry. I shall 75
often think of you and miss you. Pat will miss you too. I am leaving tomorrow."

He did not answer. When he went away, I remember that a 76
new moon hung over the mountains, and I watched him go in
silence up the hill. I expected him the next day, but he did not
come. The details of packing my personal belongings, loading
my car, arranging the bed over the seat, where the dog would
ride, occupied me until late in the day. I closed the cabin and
started the car, noticing that the sun was in the west and I should
do well to be out of the mountains by nightfall. I stopped by the
orphanage and left the cabin key and money for my light bill
with Miss Clark.

"And will you call Jerry for me to say good-by to him?"   77

"I don't know where he is," she said. "I'm afraid he's not   78
well. He didn't eat his dinner this noon. One of the other boys
saw him going over the hill into the laurel. He was supposed to
fire the boiler this afternoon. It's not like him; he's unusually
reliable."

I was almost relieved, for I knew I should never see him   79
again, and it would be easier not to say good-by to him.

I said, "I wanted to talk with you about his mother—why   80
he's here—but I'm in more of a hurry than I expected to be. It's
out of the question for me to see her now too. But here's some
money I'd like to leave with you to buy things for him at Christmas and on his birthday. It will be better than for me to try to
send him things. I could so easily duplicate—skates, for
instance."

She blinked her honest spinster's eyes.   81

"There's not much use for skates here," she said.   82

Her stupidity annoyed me.   83

"What I mean," I said, "is that I don't want to duplicate   84
things his mother sends him. I might have chosen skates if I
didn't know she had already given them to him."

She stared at me.   85

"I don't understand," she said. "He has no mother. He has   86
no skates."

 Focusing on the Story

1   Why has the narrator come to the Carolina mountains? What is her
occupation? What time of year is it? What do the mountains look like?

2   Who is Jerry and how does he meet the narrator?

3   The narrator says that Jerry has integrity. What does this term
mean?

4   One day Jerry tells the narrator something that greatly shocks her.
What does he tell her?

5   The narrator decides to go to Mannville to find out about Jerry's mother but then changes her mind. Why does she want to see the mother? Why does she change her mind?

 Interpreting and Evaluating

1   At the beginning of the story, we learn that the narrator has contracted malaria in the subtropics and later that she'll close her place in Florida and travel to Mexico and Alaska. What can you infer from these comments about the narrator's lifestyle and economic status? What else can you say about the narrator?

2   When the narrator gives Jerry little gifts of candy and apples, Jerry is speechless. Why may he have trouble saying a simple "thank-you"?

3   Why does Jerry lie about his mother? Would you call Jerry a regular liar who should be punished? Explain.

4   Why does the narrator believe Jerry so readily? Does she really understand Jerry? How would you have reacted to Jerry's story?

5   How do you think the narrator feels after she has talked to Miss Clark at the orphanage at the end of the story? What does the narrator learn about people from this experience?

 Ideas for Writing and Further Discussion

1   "A Mother in Mannville" contains some beautiful descriptive paragraphs. Reread the first page, and pay close attention to the descriptions. Then write two or three paragraphs describing a favorite place of your own at different times of the year. Start with a general sentence that expresses your feeling toward the place.

2   Does fantasy sometimes provide an important escape from a harsh reality? Write an essay about an incident in your life when your fantasy helped you cope. If you don't want to write about yourself, write about someone you know instead. What happened? How did the ability to dream or fantasize help you deal with the situation? It's not necessary to write a formal thesis statement in a narrative essay, but you may wish to start with a general statement that expresses an attitude toward the experience.

3   The author uses the anecdote about Jerry and the broken ax handle to illustrate the meaning of the word *integrity*. Choose an abstract word such as *courage, friendship,* or *maturity* that cannot be adequately defined by a simple word or phrase. Illustrate its meaning with an anecdote or a brief story. You may start by stating the dictionary definition of your word, and then tell the anecdote that illustrates what the word means to you.

4   The narrator admires Jerry for his many positive character traits. Even though he's only twelve, he appears instinctively courteous and gracious, sensitive to the needs of the narrator, independent, and mature. Write an essay in which you discuss some of his most admirable qualities and illustrate each quality with examples from the story.

   Suggested *thesis*: two or three qualities *or* two or three groups of similar qualities that the narrator admires in Jerry.

   Each *body paragraph* should illustrate one such quality (or group of related qualities) with details from the story.

5   Write an essay in which you compare and contrast the narrator and Jerry. Who is more sensitive to the needs of others? Are they both independent?

   Suggested *thesis*: two or three ways they are alike and/or different.

   Each *body paragraph* should explore one way they are alike or different.

Thank You M'am

Langston Hughes

About the Author

Langston Hughes was an African-American writer who wrote books, poems, and short stories about everyday life in Harlem. He died in 1967.

 Something to Think About

What kind of a woman would you expect to have the name Mrs. Luella Bates Washington Jones? How would you expect such a woman to treat a boy who tries to steal her purse? How can kindness change a person's behavior?

 Words to Keep in Mind

sitter *(1)* slang for buttocks
frail *(16)* thin and delicate; weak
half nelson *(22)* wrestling term

S he was a large woman with a large purse that had every- 1
thing in it but a hammer and nails. It had a long strap, and she carried it slung across her shoulder. It was about eleven

o'clock at night, dark, and she was walking alone, when a boy ran up behind her and tried to snatch her purse. The strap broke with the sudden single tug the boy gave it from behind. But the boy's weight and the weight of the purse combined caused him to lose his balance. Instead of taking off full blast as he had hoped, the boy fell on his back on the sidewalk and his legs flew up. The large woman simply turned around and kicked him right square in his blue-jeaned sitter. Then she reached down, picked the boy up by his shirt front, and shook him until his teeth rattled.

After that the woman said, "Pick up my pocketbook, boy, and give it here." 2

She still held him tightly. But she bent down enough to permit him to stoop and pick up her purse. Then she said, "Now ain't you ashamed of yourself?" 3

Firmly gripped by his shirt front, the boy said, "Yes'm." 4

The woman said, "What did you want to do it for?" 5

The boy said, "I didn't aim to." 6

She said, "You a lie!" 7

By that time two or three people passed, stopped, turned to look, and some stood watching. 8

"If I turn you loose, will you run?" asked the woman. 9

"Yes'm," said the boy. 10

"Then I won't turn you loose," said the woman. She did not release him. 11

"Lady, I'm sorry," whispered the boy. 12

"Um-hum! Your face is dirty. I got a great mind to wash your face for you. Ain't you got nobody home to tell you to wash your face?" 13

"No'm," said the boy. 14

"Then it will get washed this evening," said the large woman, starting up the street, dragging the frightened boy behind her. 15

He looked as if he were fourteen or fifteen, frail and willow-wild, in tennis shoes and blue jeans. 16

The woman said, "You ought to be my son. I would teach you right from wrong. Least I can do right now is to wash your face. Are you hungry?" 17

"No'm," said the being-dragged boy. "I just want you to turn 18
me loose."

"Was I bothering *you* when I turned that corner?" asked the 19
woman.

"No'm." 20

"But you put yourself in contact with *me*," said the woman. 21
"If you think that that contact is not going to last a while, you
got another thought coming. When I get through with you, sir,
you are going to remember Mrs. Luella Bates Washington
Jones."

Sweat popped out on the boy's face and he began to strug- 22
gle. Mrs. Jones stopped, jerked him around in front of her, put a
half nelson about his neck, and continued to drag him up the
street. When she got to her door, she dragged the boy inside,
down a hall, and into a large kitchenette-furnished room at the
rear of the house. She switched on the light and left the door
open. The boy could hear other roomers laughing and talking in
the large house. Some of their doors were open, too, so he knew
he and the woman were not alone. The woman still had him by
the neck in the middle of her room.

She said, "What is your name?" 23

"Roger," answered the boy. 24

"Then, Roger, you go to that sink and wash your face," said 25
the woman, whereupon she turned him loose—at last. Roger
looked at the door—looked at the woman—looked at the door—
and went to the sink.

"Let the water run until it gets warm," she said. "Here's a 26
clean towel."

"You gonna take me to jail?" asked the boy, bending over the 27
sink.

"Not with that face, I would not take you nowhere," said the 28
woman. "Here I am trying to get home to cook me a bite to eat,
and you snatch my pocketbook! Maybe you ain't been to your
supper either, late as it be. Have you?"

"There's nobody home at my house," said the boy. 29

"Then we'll eat," said the woman. "I believe you're hun- 30
gry—or been hungry—to try to snatch my pocketbook!"

"I want a pair of blue suede shoes," said the boy. 31

"Well, you didn't have to snatch *my* pocketbook to get some   32
suede shoes," said Mrs. Luella Bates Washington Jones. "You
could of asked me."

"M'am?"   33

The water dripping from his face, the boy looked at her. There   34
was a long pause. A very long pause. After he had dried his face,
and not knowing what else to do, dried it again, the boy turned
around, wondering what next. The door was open. He could
make a dash for it down the hall. He could run, run, run, *run!*

The woman was sitting on the daybed. After a while she   35
said, "I were young once and I wanted things I could not get."

There was another long pause. The boy's mouth opened.   36
Then he frowned, not knowing he frowned.

The woman said, "Um-hum! You thought I was going to say   37
but, didn't you? You thought I was going to say, *but I didn't
snatch people's pocketbooks.* Well, I wasn't going to say that."
Pause. Silence. "I have done things, too, which I would not tell
you, son—neither tell God, if He didn't already know. Everybody's got something in common. So you set down while I fix us
something to eat. You might run that comb through your hair so
you will look presentable."

In another corner of the room behind a screen was a gas   38
plate and an icebox. Mrs. Jones got up and went behind the
screen. The woman did not watch the boy to see if he was going
to run now, nor did she watch her purse, which she left behind
her on the daybed. But the boy took care to sit on the far side of
the room, away from the purse, where be thought she could easily see him out of the corner of her eye if she wanted to. He did
not trust the woman *not* to trust him. And he did not want to be
mistrusted now.

"Do you need somebody to go to the store," asked the boy,   39
"maybe to get some milk or something?"

"Don't believe I do," said the woman, "unless you just want   40
sweet milk yourself. I was going to make cocoa out of this
canned milk I got here."

"That will be fine," said the boy.   41

She heated some lima beans and ham she had in the icebox,   42
made the cocoa, and set the table. The woman did not ask the

boy anything about where he lived, or his folks, or anything else that would embarrass him. Instead, as they ate, she told him about her job in a hotel beauty shop that stayed open late, what the work was like, and how all kinds of women came in and out, blondes, redheads, and Spanish. Then she cut him a half of her ten cent cake.

"Eat some more, son," she said.   43

When they were finished eating, she got up and said, "Now   44 here, take this ten dollars and buy yourself some blue suede shoes. And next time, do not make the mistake of latching onto my pocketbook *nor nobody else's*—because shoes got by devilish ways will burn your feet. I got to get my rest now. But from here on in, son, I hope you will behave yourself."

She led him down the hall to the front door and opened it.   45 "Good night! Behave yourself, boy!" she said, looking out into the street as he went down the steps.

The boy wanted to say something other than, "Thank you,   46 m'am," to Mrs. Luella Bates Washington Jones, but although his lips moved, he couldn't even say that as he turned at the foot of the barren stoop and looked up at the large woman in the door. Then she shut the door.

 Focusing on the Story

1   Describe the two characters in the story, Mrs. Luella Bates Washington Jones and Roger. Why are they both out on the street at eleven o'clock at night?

2   Why doesn't Roger run away after he tries to snatch Mrs. Jones's purse?

3   Describe Mrs. Jones's apartment. Does she have a lot of money? What does Roger need money for?

 Interpreting and Evaluating

1   Although Roger has tried to steal her purse, Mrs. Jones drags the boy home with her. Why doesn't she call the police?

2 Why doesn't Roger run away when Mrs. Jones finally turns him loose in the apartment? Why doesn't he "want to be mistrusted now"?

3 What kind of family life does Roger appear to have? Point to evidence in the story to support your view. Why can't he ask his parents for money?

4 Mrs. Jones says that she was "young once and . . . wanted things [she] couldn't get" and that she had "done things, too, that she couldn't tell." What may her childhood have been like? How may Mrs. Jones's childhood have been similar to Roger's?

5 Does Mrs. Jones do the right thing by rewarding Roger? Should Roger have been punished?

6 Why does Roger have trouble saying "thank you" at the end of the story? Do you think he has had much occasion to use this phrase? Explain.

7 Mrs. Jones says that Roger is "going to remember Mrs. Luella Bates Washington Jones." Why will Roger probably remember her? How do you think this episode will affect Roger's life and criminal activities?

 Ideas for Writing and Further Discussion

1 Most of us would probably agree that we need more people like Mrs. Luella Bates Washington Jones. What are some of Mrs. Jones's personality traits that cause her to have an impact on Roger? Write an essay in which you discuss two or three of Mrs. Jones's positive traits (or two or three groups of similar traits), and show how and why these traits have an impact on Roger.

Suggested *thesis*: two or three of Mrs. Jones's positive traits (or two or three groups of related traits).

Each *body paragraph* should discuss one trait or group of related traits.

2 What are some causes of crime? Write an essay in which you discuss several major causes of crime as shown in the story.

Suggested *thesis*: several causes of crime.

Each *body paragraph* should explore one of the causes of crime.

3 Is incarceration—putting people in jail—the only way to reduce crime? Write an essay in which you discuss some ways to reduce crime.

Suggested *thesis*: two or three ways to reduce crime.

Each *body paragraph* should explore one way.

4   Can criminals be rehabilitated? Write an essay in which you discuss some ways to rehabilitate young criminal offenders.

Suggested *thesis*: two or three ways to rehabilitate young criminal offenders.

Each *body paragraph* should look at one such way.

 Additional Ideas for Discussion and Writing

1   Although the woman (the writer who tells the story) in "A Mother in Mannville" by Marjorie Rawlings is educated, well-off, and white, she possesses little insight in basic human behavior. On the other hand, although Mrs. Luella Bates Washington Jones in "Thank You M'am" by Langston Hughes is uneducated, poor, and black, she is wise and knows quite a bit about human nature.

Write an essay in which you compare and contrast the writer in "A Mother in Mannville" and Mrs. Luella Bates Washington Jones in "Thank You M'am." Choose several areas or categories to compare and contrast, focusing on clear and striking contrasts such as education and life experience. Illustrate your points with examples from the two stories. In the conclusion, you may state which character is more perceptive and has the keenest wit.

Suggested *thesis*: three or four categories to compare and/or contrast.

Each *body paragraph* should explore one category or group of similar categories.

2   Compare and contrast Jerry, the orphan boy in "A Mother in Mannville" by Marjorie Rawlings and Mrs. Luella Bates Washington Jones in "Thank You M'am" by Langston Hughes. Focus on unexpected similarities. For example, even though Jerry is young, he is mature and wise, and, like Mrs. Luella Bates Washington Jones, has learned to cope with his situation in life. Overall then, like Mrs. Luella Bates Washington Jones, he may be able to impact others.

Suggested *thesis*: several areas or categories to compare and contrast.

Each *body paragraph* should explore one area or category and give examples from the stories to illustrate each point.

The Stolen Party

Liliana Heker

About the Author

Liliana Heker, born in 1942, is an Argentine writer who published her first volume of short stories, *Those Who Beheld the Burning Bush*, while still in her teens. Later she became editor-in-chief of the literary magazine *El Ornitorrinco*, a forum for writers during the years of Argentina's brutal military dictatorships. Her novel, *Zona de Clivage*, won the Buenos Aires Municipal Prize.

 ### Something to Think About

How do children and adults differ in their views of others? What do children admire in other children? On what do adults often base their views and attitudes toward others? What causes people to become more cynical and question the sincerity of those around them?

 ### Words to Keep in Mind

pompously *(11)* proudly, self-importantly

charades *(38)* game of guessing a word by pantomiming or expressing the word or its syllables by gestures

 As soon as she arrived she went straight to the kitchen to see if the monkey was there. It was: what a relief! She

---

wouldn't have liked to admit that her mother had been right. *Monkeys at a birthday?* her mother had sneered. *Get away with you, believing any nonsense you're told!* She was cross, but not because of the monkey, the girl thought; it's just because of the party.

"I don't like you going," she told her. "It's a rich people's 2 party."

"Rich people go to Heaven too," said the girl, who studied 3 religion at school.

"Get away with Heaven," said the mother. "The problem 4 with you, young lady, is that you like to fart higher than your ass."

The girl didn't approve of the way her mother spoke. She 5 was barely nine, and one of the best in her class.

"I'm going because I've been invited," she said. "And I've 6 been invited because Luciana is my friend. So there."

"Ah yes, your friend," her mother grumbled. She paused. 7 "Listen, Rosaura," she said at last. "That one's not your friend. You know what you are to them? The maid's daughter, that's what."

Rosaura blinked hard: she wasn't going to cry. Then she 8 yelled: "Shut up! You know nothing about being friends!"

Every afternoon she used to go to Luciana's house and they 9 would both finish their homework while Rosaura's mother did the cleaning. They had their tea in the kitchen and they told each other secrets. Rosaura loved everything in the big house, and she also loved the people who lived there.

"I'm going because it will be the most lovely party in the 10 whole world, Luciana told me it would. There will be a magician, and he will bring a monkey and everything."

The mother swung around to take a good look at her child, 11 and pompously put her hands on her hips.

"Monkeys at a birthday?" she said. "Get away with you, 12 believing any nonsense you're told!"

Rosaura was deeply offended. She thought it unfair of her 13 mother to accuse other people of being liars simply because they were rich. Rosaura too wanted to be rich, of course. If one day she managed to live in a beautiful palace, would her mother stop loving her? She felt very sad. She wanted to go to that party more than anything else in the world.

"I'll die if I don't go," she whispered, almost without moving her lips.   14

And she wasn't sure whether she had been heard, but on the morning of the party she discovered that her mother had starched her Christmas dress. And in the afternoon, after washing her hair, her mother rinsed it in apple vinegar so that it would be all nice and shiny. Before going out, Rosaura admired herself in the mirror, with her white dress and glossy hair, and thought she looked terribly pretty.   15

Señora Ines also seemed to notice. As soon as she saw her, she said: 16

"How lovely you look today, Rosaura."   17

Rosaura gave her starched skirt a slight toss with her hands and walked into the party with a firm step. She said hello to Luciana and asked about the monkey. Luciana put on a secretive look and whispered into Rosaura's ear: "He's in the kitchen. But don't tell anyone, because it's a surprise."   18

Rosaura wanted to make sure. Carefully she entered the kitchen and there she saw it: deep in thought, inside its cage. It looked so funny that the girl stood there for a while, watching it, and later, every so often, she would slip out of the party unseen and go and admire it. Rosaura was the only one allowed into the kitchen. Señora Ines had said: "You yes, but not the others, they're much too boisterous, they might break something." Rosaura had never broken anything. She even managed the jug of orange juice, carrying it from the kitchen into the dining room. She held it carefully and didn't spill a single drop. And Señora Ines had said: "Are you sure you can manage a jug as big as that?" Of course she could manage. She wasn't a butterfingers, like the others. Like that blonde girl with the bow in her hair. As soon as she saw Rosaura, the girl with the bow had said: 19

"And you? Who are you?"   20

"I'm a friend of Luciana," said Rosaura.   21

"No," said the girl with the bow, "you are not a friend of 22
Luciana because I'm her cousin and I know all her friends. And I
don't know you."

"So what," said Rosaura. "I come here every afternoon with 23
my mother and we do our homework together."

"You and your mother do your homework together?" asked 24
the girl, laughing.

"I and Luciana do our homework together," said Rosaura, 25
very seriously.

The girl with the bow shrugged her shoulders. 26

"That's not being friends," she said. "Do you go to school 27
together?"

"No." 28

"So where do you know her from?" said the girl, getting 29
impatient.

Rosaura remembered her mother's words perfectly. She took 30
a deep breath.

"I'm the daughter of the employee," she said. 31

Her mother had said very clearly: "If someone asks, you say 32
you're the daughter of the employee; that's all." She also told
her to add: "And proud of it." But Rosaura thought that never in
her life would she dare say something of the sort.

"What employee?" said the girl with the bow. "Employee in 30
a shop?"

"No," said Rosaura angrily. "My mother doesn't sell any- 34
thing in any shop, so there."

"So how come she's an employee?" said the girl with the 35
bow.

Just then Señora Ines arrived saying *shh shh*, and asked 36
Rosaura if she wouldn't mind helping serve out the hotdogs, as
she knew the house so much better than the others.

"See?" said Rosaura to the girl with the bow, and when no 37
one was looking she kicked her in the shin.

Apart from the girl with the bow, all the others were delight- 38
ful. The one she liked best was Luciana, with her golden birthday
crown; and then the boys. Rosaura won the sack race, and nobody
managed to catch her when they played tag. When they split into

two teams to play charades, all the boys wanted her for their side. Rosaura felt she had never been so happy in all her life.

But the best was still to come. The best came after Luciana 39 blew out the candles. First the cake. Señora Ines had asked her to help pass the cake around, and Rosaura had enjoyed the task immensely, because everyone called out to her, shouting "Me, me!" Rosaura remembered a story in which there was a queen who had the power of life or death over her subjects. She had always loved that, having the power of life or death. To Luciana and the boys she gave the largest pieces, and to the girl with the bow she gave a slice so thin one could see through it.

After the cake came the magician, tall and bony, with a fine 40 red cape. A true magician: he could untie handkerchiefs by blowing on them and make a chain with links that had no openings. He could guess what cards were pulled out from a pack, and the monkey was his assistant. He called the monkey "partner." "Let's see here, partner," he would say, "turn over a card." And, "Don't run away, partner: time to work now."

The final trick was wonderful. One of the children had to 41 hold the monkey in his arms and the magician said he would make him disappear.

"What, the boy?" they all shouted. 42

"No, the monkey!" shouted back the magician. 43

Rosaura thought that this was truly the most amusing party 44 in the whole world.

The magician asked a small fat boy to come and help, but the 45 small fat boy got frightened almost at once and dropped the monkey on the floor. The magician picked him up carefully, whispered something in his ear, and the monkey nodded almost as if he understood.

"You mustn't be so unmanly, my friend," the magician said 46 to the fat boy.

"What's unmanly?" said the fat boy. 47

The magician turned around as if to look for spies. 48

"A sissy," said the magician. "Go sit down." 49

Then he stared at all the faces, one by one. Rosaura felt her 50 heart tremble.

"You, with the Spanish eyes," said the magician. And every-   51
one saw that he was pointing at her.

She wasn't afraid. Neither holding the monkey, nor when   52
the magician made him vanish; not even when, at the end, the
magician flung his red cape over Rosaura's head and uttered a
few magic words . . . and the monkey reappeared, chattering
happily, in her arms. The children clapped furiously. And before
Rosaura returned to her seat, the magician said:

"Thank you very much, my little countess."   53

She was so pleased with the compliment that a while later,   54
when her mother came to fetch her, that was the first thing she
told her.

"I helped the magician and he said to me, 'Thank you very   55
much, my little countess.'"

It was strange because up to then Rosaura had thought that   56
she was angry with her mother. All along Rosaura had imagined
that she would say to her: "See that the monkey wasn't a lie?"
But instead she was so thrilled that she told her mother all about
the wonderful magician.

Her mother tapped her on the head and said: "So now we're   57
a countess!"

But one could see that she was beaming.   58

And now they both stood in the entrance, because a moment   59
ago Señora Ines, smiling, had said: "Please wait here a second."

Her mother suddenly seemed worried.   60

"What is it?" she asked Rosaura.   61

"What is what?" said Rosaura. "It's nothing; she just wants   62
to get the presents for those who are leaving, see?"

She pointed at the fat boy and at a girl with pigtails who   63
were also waiting there, next to their mothers. And she explained about the presents. She knew, because she had been
watching those who left before her. When one of the girls was
about to leave, Señora Ines would give her a bracelet. When a
boy left, Señora Ines gave him a yo-yo. Rosaura preferred the
yo-yo because it sparkled, but she didn't mention that to her
mother. Her mother might have said: "So why don't you ask for
one, you blockhead?" That's what her mother was like. Rosaura

didn't feel like explaining that she'd be horribly ashamed to be the odd one out. Instead she said:

"I was the best-behaved at the party."   64

And she said no more because Señora Ines came out into the   65
hall with two bags, one pink and one blue.

First she went up to the fat boy, gave him a yo-yo out of the   66
blue bag, and the fat boy left with his mother. Then she went up
to the girl and gave her a bracelet out of the pink bag, and the
girl with the pigtails left as well.

Finally she came up to Rosaura and her mother. She had a   67
big smile on her face and Rosaura liked that. Señora Ines looked
down at her, then looked up at her mother, and then said something that made Rosaura proud:

"What a marvelous daughter you have, Herminia."   68

For an instant, Rosaura thought that she'd give her two pres-   69
ents: the bracelet and the yo-yo. Señora Ines bent down as if
about to look for something. Rosaura also leaned forward,
stretching out her arm. But she never completed the movement.

Señora Ines didn't look in the pink bag. Nor did she look in   70
the blue bag. Instead she rummaged in her purse. In her hand
appeared two bills.

"You really and truly earned this," she said handing them   71
over. "Thank you for all your help, my pet."

Rosaura felt her arms stiffen, stick close to her body, and   72
then she noticed her mother's hand on her shoulder. Instinctively she pressed herself against her mother's body. That was
all. Except her eyes. Rosaura's eyes had a cold, clear look that
fixed itself on Señora Ines's face.

Señora Ines, motionless, stood there with her hand out-   73
stretched. As if she didn't dare draw it back. As if the slightest
change might shatter an infinitely delicate balance.

Focusing on the Story

1   Describe Rosaura. How does her attitude differ from that of her mother? How and why is this difference established at the beginning of the story?

2   Why doesn't the mother want Rosaura to go to the birthday party? Doesn't she want her daughter to be happy?

3   Do Rosaura and Luciana attend the same school? Why do they do their homework together?

4   How does Rosaura feel about herself? Does she like helping Señora Ines serve orange juice, hotdogs, and cake? How does she get along with the other children at the party?

5   What do the other children receive when they leave the party? What does Rosaura get? Why does Señora Ines distinguish between Rosaura and the other children?

 Interpreting and Evaluating

1   What does the title "The Stolen Party" refer to? Who "stole" the party and in what ways?

2   How do you think Rosaura's home life differs from Luciana's? How would a birthday party in Rosaura's neighborhood differ from Luciana's party?

3   When Señora Ines hands Rosaura the money, Rosaura feels "her arms stiffen." Why doesn't Rosaura like being paid for helping Señora Ines? How would you have felt if you had been in Rosaura's place?

4   At the end of the story, Señora Ines "stood there with her hand outstretched . . . as if the slightest change might shatter an infinitely delicate balance." What is this "delicate balance"?

5   What do you think Rosaura's prospects are in life? To what extent will her social class limit her options? Do you think Luciana will continue to invite Rosaura to her house when she reaches high school and college? Why or why not? What comment does the story make on the division of social classes in Argentina?

Ideas for Writing and Further Discussion

1   At the beginning of the story, the author focuses on the conflict between Rosaura and her mother. What's another more important conflict in the short story? In two or three paragraphs, explore the two conflicts in the story. Which one is resolved?

2   At the end of the story, Rosaura has lost some of her innocence or naïveté. Like her mother, she'll probably become more skeptical and less likely to believe in the goodness of others. Think of an incident when you became more cynical and discovered the phoniness in others. Write about a time when such a change occurred in you. Describe what happened. What did somebody say or do? How did it affect you, and why do you think it affected you that way?

It's not necessary to write a formal thesis statement in a narrative essay, but you may wish to start with a general statement that expresses your attitude toward the experience.

3   In a few paragraphs, describe your relationship with your mother and compare it to either or both of the mother-daughter pairs in the story. Do you feel that your mother, like Rosaura's mother, keeps reminding you of your limitations such as age, intelligence, and background, or does she encourage you to break such boundaries?

The Open Window

Saki

About the Author

Born in Burma, Saki, whose real name was Hector Hugh Munro, was a Scottish novelist and short story writer who took the name Saki from an old Persian poem. His inventive and imaginative stories often satirize British society.

 ### Something to Think About

Have you ever played a prank on somebody? When is a prank no longer a prank?

 ### Words to Keep in Mind

endeavored *(2)* tried

rectory *(5)* the house in which a minister or priest lives

moor *(13)* open wasteland, often wet and covered with heather (British)

snipe *(13)* long-billed wading bird that lives in marshy places

bog *(13)* a small marsh

engulfed *(13)* swallowed up; absorbed completely

treacherous *(13)* dangerous; not to be trusted

marshes *(17)* low, soft lands, temporarily or permanently covered with water

delusion *(18)* a false opinion sometimes resulting from mental illness

ailments *(18)* illnesses

infirmities *(18)* weaknesses

imminent *(23)* likely to happen right away

Ganges *(26)* river in North India and Bangladesh
pariah dogs *(26)* wild, despised animals

My aunt will be down presently, Mr. Nuttel," said a 1
very self-possessed young lady of fifteen; "in the
meantime you must try and put up with me."

Framton Nuttel endeavored to say the correct something 2
which should duly flatter the niece of the moment without
unduly discounting the aunt that was to come. Privately he
doubted more than ever whether these formal visits on a succes-
sion of total strangers would do much towards helping the
nerve cure which he was supposed to be undergoing.

"I know how it will be," his sister had said when he was 3
preparing to migrate to this rural retreat; "you will bury yourself down there and not speak to a living soul, and your nerves
will be worse than ever from moping. I shall just give you letters of introduction to all the people I know there. Some of
them, as far as I can remember, were quite nice." Framton wondered whether Mrs. Sappleton, the lady to whom he was pre-
senting one of the letters of introduction, came into the nice
division.

"Do you know many of the people round here?" asked the 4
niece, when she judged that they had had sufficient silent communion.

"Hardly a soul," said Framton. "My sister was staying here, 5
at the rectory, you know, some four years ago, and she gave me
letters of introduction to some of the people here."

He made the last statement in a tone of distinct regret. 6

"Then you know practically nothing about my aunt?" pur- 7
sued the self-possessed young lady.

"Only her name and address," admitted the caller. He was 8
wondering whether Mrs. Sappleton was in the married or wid-

owed state. An undefinable something about the room seemed
to suggest masculine habitation.

"Her great tragedy happened just three years ago," said the 9
child; "that would be since your sister's time."

"Her tragedy?" asked Framton; somehow in this restful 10
country spot tragedies seemed out of place.

"You may wonder why we keep that window wide open on 11
an October afternoon," said the niece, indicating a large French
window that opened onto a lawn.

"It is quite warm for the time of the year," said Framton; 12
"but has that window got anything to do with the tragedy?"

"Out through that window, three years ago to a day, her hus- 13
band and her two young brothers went off for their day's shooting. They never came back. In crossing the moor to their favorite
snipe-shooting ground they were all three engulfed in a treacherous piece of bog. It had been that dreadful wet summer, you
know, and places that were safe in other years gave way suddenly without warning. Their bodies were never recovered. That
was the dreadful part of it." Here the child's voice lost its self-
possessed note and became falteringly human. "Poor aunt
always thinks that they will come back some day, they and the
little brown spaniel that was lost with them, and walk in at that
window just as they used to do. That is why the window is kept
open every evening till it is quite dusk. Poor dear aunt, she has
often told me how they went out, her husband with his white
waterproof coat over his arm, and Ronnie, her youngest brother,
singing, 'Bertie, why do you bound?' as he always did to tease
her, because she said it got on her nerves. Do you know, sometimes on still, quiet evenings like this, I almost get a creepy feeling that they will all walk in through that window—"

She broke off with a little shudder. It was a relief to Framton 14
when the aunt bustled into the room with a whirl of apologies
for being late in making her appearance.

"I hope Vera has been amusing you?" she said. 15

"She has been very interesting," said Framton. 16

"I hope you don't mind the open window," said Mrs. Sap- 17
pleton briskly; "my husband and brothers will be home directly

from shooting, and they always come in this way. They've been out for snipe in the marshes today, so they'll make a fine mess over my poor carpets. So like you menfolk, isn't it?" She rattled on cheerfully about the shooting and the scarcity of birds, and the prospects for duck in the winter. To Framton it was all purely horrible. He made a desperate effort to turn the talk onto a less ghastly topic; he was conscious that his hostess was giving him only a fragment of her attention, and her eyes were constantly straying past him to the open window and the lawn beyond. It was certainly an unfortunate coincidence that he should have paid his visit on this tragic anniversary.

"The doctors agree in ordering me complete rest, an absence   18
of mental excitement, and avoidance of any violent physical exercise," announced Framton, who labored under the tolerably widespread delusion that total strangers and chance acquaintances are hungry for the least detail of one's ailments and infirmities. "On the matter of diet they are not so much in agreement," he continued.

"No?" said Mrs. Sappleton, in a voice which only replaced a   19
yawn at the last moment. Then she suddenly brightened into alert attention—but not to what Framton was saying.

"Here they are at last!" she cried. "Just in time for tea, and   20
don't they look as if they were muddy up to the eyes!"

Framton shivered slightly and turned towards the niece with   21
a look intended to convey sympathetic comprehension. The child was staring out through the open window with dazed horror in her eyes. In a chill shock of nameless fear Framton swung round in his seat and looked in the same direction.

In the deepening twilight three figures were walking across   22
the lawn towards the window; they all carried guns under their arms, and one of them was additionally burdened with a white coat hung over his shoulders. A tired brown spaniel kept close at their heels. Noiselessly they neared the house, and then a hoarse young voice chanted out of the dusk: "I said, Bertie, why do you bound?"

Framton grabbed wildly at his stick and hat; the hall door,   23
the gravel drive, and the front gate were dimly noted stages in

his headlong retreat. A cyclist coming along the road had to run into the hedge to avoid imminent collision.

"Here we are, my dear," said the bearer of the white mackin-   24
tosh, coming in through the window; "fairly muddy, but most of it's dry. Who was that who bolted out as we came up?"

"A most extraordinary man, a Mr. Nuttel," said Mrs. Sapple-   25
ton; "could only talk about his illnesses, and dashed off without a word of good-by or apology when you arrived. One would think he had seen a ghost."

"I expect it was the spaniel," said the niece calmly; "he told   26
me he had a horror of dogs. He was once hunted into a cemetery somewhere on the banks of the Ganges by a pack of pariah dogs, and had to spend the night in a newly dug grave with the creatures snarling and grinning and foaming just above him. Enough to make anyone lose their nerve."

Romance at short notice was her speciality.   27

 Focusing on the Story

1   Why has Framton Nuttel come to stay in the English countryside?

2   According to Vera, the niece, what was the tragedy that was supposed to have happened three years ago? Did it really happen?

3   Vera, Mrs. Sappleton's niece, is described as "a very self-possessed young lady of fifteen." What other words could be used to describe her?

4   Why does Framton Nuttel grab "wildly at his stick and hat" and bolt out the door? What does he think he has seen coming through the open window? Who is really coming through the window?

5   How does Vera, the niece, explain Mr. Nuttel's sudden departure?

 Interpreting and Evaluating

1   How does the name Framton Nuttel reflect Mr. Nuttel's character?

2   In what ways is Framton Nuttel different from the niece?

3   Why does Vera tell Framton Nuttel such a bizarre story, and why does Framton believe it?

4   The author uses some very formal words and phrases such as *endeavor, sufficient silent communion,* and *masculine habitation,* in addition to some overly long sentences. What effect does such formal language have on the story? How does it contribute to the humor? What does Saki ridicule in this story?

5   The last sentence, "Romance at short notice was her speciality," refers to the niece. What does it mean? Could the statement also refer to the author? Explain.

 Ideas for Writing and Further Discussion

1   Write about a time when you played a prank on someone. What did you do? Who was the butt of your joke? How do you think he or she felt? What would you have done if the prank had backfired?

2   Write about a time when someone played a prank on you. Who was your tormentor or prankster? What happened? How did it make you feel?

It's not necessary to write a formal thesis statement in a narrative essay, but you may wish to start with a general sentence that introduces the event and expresses your attitude toward the incident.

The Little Match Girl

Hans Christian Andersen

About the Author

Hans Christian Andersen was the son of a poor shoemaker and grew up in a small town in Denmark in the 1800s. At that time, the Scandinavian countries were among the poorest in Europe. Andersen's stories, whose characters are mostly poor, were read by almost everyone, even the kings and queens. Soon people started to demand a change in the social system. Today the Scandinavian countries have the highest standard of living in the world. Other famous stories by Andersen include "The Emperor's New Clothes," "The Little Mermaid," and "The Ugly Duckling."

 Something to Think About

Can dramatic fiction about social problems help correct social ills? Hans Christian Andersen's stories were read by the kings and queens in Scandinavia. What impact may the following story have had on them?

It was so terribly cold. Snow was falling, and it was almost dark. Evening came on, the last evening of the year. In the cold and gloom a poor little girl, bareheaded and barefoot, was walking through the streets. Of course when she had left her house she'd had slippers on, but what good had they been? They were very big slippers, way too big for her, for they belonged to her mother. The little girl had lost them running across the road, where two carriages had rattled by terribly fast. One slipper she'd not been able to find again, and a boy had run off with the other, saying he could use it very well as a cradle some day when he had children of his own. And so the little girl walked on her naked feet, which were quite red and blue with the cold. In an old apron she carried several packages of matches, and she held a box of them in her hand. No one had bought any from her all day long, and no one had given her a cent.

Shivering with cold and hunger, she crept along, a picture of misery, poor little girl! The snowflakes fell on her long fair hair, which hung in pretty curls over her neck. But she didn't think of her pretty curls now. In all the windows lights were shining, and there was a wonderful smell of roast goose, for it was New Year's Eve. Yes, she thought of that! 2

In a corner formed by two houses, one of which projected farther out into the street than the other, she sat down and drew up her little feet under her. She was getting colder and colder, but did not dare to go home, for she had sold no matches, nor earned a single cent, and her father would surely beat her. Besides, it was cold at home, for they had nothing over them but a roof through which the wind whistled even though the biggest cracks had been stuffed with straw and rags. 3

Her hands were almost dead with cold. Oh, how much one little match might warm her! If she could only take one from the box and rub it against the wall and warm her hands. She drew one out. *R-r-ratch!* How it sputtered and burned! It made a warm, bright flame, like a little candle, as she held her hands over it; but it gave a strange light! It really seemed to the little girl as if she were sitting before a great iron stove with shining brass knobs and a brass cover. How wonderfully the fire burned! How comfortable it was! The youngster stretched out her feet to warm them too; then the little flame went out, the stove vanished, and she had only the remains of the burnt match in her hand. 4

She struck another match against the wall. It burned brightly, 5
and when the light fell upon the wall it became transparent like a
thin veil, and she could see through it into a room. On the table a
snow-white cloth was spread, and on it stood a shining dinner service. The roast goose steamed gloriously, stuffed with apples and
prunes. And what was still better, the goose jumped down from
the dish and waddled along the floor, with a knife and fork in its
breast, right over to the little girl. Then the match went out, and
she could see only the thick, cold wall. She lighted another match.
Then she was sitting under the most beautiful Christmas tree. It
was much larger and much more beautiful than the one she had
seen last Christmas through the glass door at the rich merchant's
home. Thousands of candles burned on the green branches, and
colored pictures like those in the printshops looked down at her.
The little girl reached both her hands toward them. Then the
match went out. But the Christmas lights mounted higher. She
saw them now as bright stars in the sky. One of them fell down,
forming a long line of fire.

"Now someone is dying," thought the little girl, for her old 6
grandmother, the only person who had loved her, and who was
now dead, had told her that when a star fell down a soul went
up to God.

She rubbed another match against the wall. It became bright 7
again, and in the glow the old grandmother stood clear and
shining, kind and lovely.

"Grandmother!" cried the child. "Oh, take me with you! I 8
know you will disappear when the match is burned out. You
will vanish like the warm stove, the wonderful roast goose and
the beautiful big Christmas tree!"

And she quickly struck the whole bundle of matches, for she 9
wished to keep her grandmother with her. And the matches
burned with such a glow that it became brighter than daylight.
Grandmother had never been so grand and beautiful. She took
the little girl in her arms, and both of them flew in brightness
and joy above the earth, very, very high, and up there was neither cold, nor hunger, nor fear—they were with God.

But in the corner, leaning against the wall, sat the little girl 10 with red cheeks and smiling mouth, frozen to death on the last evening of the old year. The New Year's sun rose upon a little pathetic figure. The child sat there, stiff and cold, holding the matches, of which one bundle was almost burned.

"She wanted to warm herself," the people said. No one 11 imagined what beautiful things she had seen, and how happily she had gone with her old grandmother into the bright New Year.

 Focusing on the Story

1   Describe the little girl as she's walking through the cold streets. About how old is she? What has happened to her shoes?

2   Describe the setting (time and place) of the story.

3   How does the little girl feel? Why is she unable to go home? Why does she burn all her matches, and what does she "see" in the burning flames?

4   What do people see the next morning, New Year's Day? What do they say when they see the burned matches?

 Interpreting and Evaluating

1   What is the author's attitude toward the little girl? In other words, what is the story's tone? What words and phrases has the author chosen to convey this attitude or tone? Do you feel sympathy for the girl?

2   Describe your own feelings as you were reading the three last paragraphs of the story. What accounts for the strong emotional impact (the story's mood) of the ending?

3   How would you react if you came across the little girl, frozen to death, holding her burned matches?

4   Does anyone in our society today remind you of the little match girl? If so, who?

5   It has been said that the poor will always be with us. Do you agree with this statement? What can be done to prevent poverty?

Ideas for Writing and Further Discussion

Andersen writes that the little girl "did not dare to go home, for she had sold no matches, nor earned a single cent, and her father would surely beat her." Could such blatant child neglect or abuse occur in our society today? Are child abuse and poverty connected? Do you know of any place where child labor still exists?

1   Write an essay in which you explore reasons why child abuse occurs. Use examples from your own experience or from research to illustrate your points.

Suggested *thesis*: two or three reasons why child abuse occurs in certain families or areas.

Each *body paragraph* should explore one cause and give examples that illustrate how that one cause leads to child abuse.

2   Write an essay in which you discuss several steps that have been taken to prevent child labor and hunger in our own country.

Suggested *thesis*: two or three social programs that help alleviate each of these social ills.

Each *body paragraph* should explore one program and show how it alleviates social problems.

 An Additional Idea for Discussion and Writing

Discuss or write an essay in which you compare and contrast Jerry, the orphan boy in "A Mother in Mannville" by Marjorie Rawlings, and the little girl in "The Little Match Girl" by Hans Christian Andersen. How are they similar? How do they differ? For example, do they both resort to illusion and fantasy to deal with their harsh realities? How do their illusions differ? What are the results of their dreams?

Suggested *thesis*: two or three areas (categories) they are similar or different.

Each *body paragraph* should explore one area or category and include examples from the stories to illustrate each point.

Charles

Shirley Jackson

About the Author

Shirley Jackson was an American novelist and short story writer who grew up in California. Many of her works have been adapted for radio and television. Her most famous short story, "The Lottery," a contemporary horror story, appears in many anthologies. She has also written many novels, including *The Haunting of Hill House*. She died in 1965.

 Something to Think About

It's often difficult to take responsibility for our own actions. Have you ever blamed somebody else for something you did?

 Words to Keep in Mind

renounced *(1)* gave up

tot *(1)* small child

swaggering *(1)* arrogant, showing off

raucous *(2)* loud and rowdy

insolently *(3)* disrespectfully

pounding *(20)* banging or hitting hard

deprived *(20)* kept from having

scornfully *(33)* full of contempt

scanning *(63)* looking at closely in a searching way

matronly *(63)* like a mature woman

primly *(68)* stiffly formal

lapses *(68)* slips or falls

T he day my son Laurie started kindergarten he re- 1
nounced corduroy overalls with bibs and began wearing blue jeans with a belt; I watched him go off the first morning
with the older girl next door, seeing clearly that an era of my life
was ended, my sweet-voiced nursery-school tot replaced by a
long-trousered, swaggering character who forgot to stop at the
corner and wave good-bye to me.

He came home the same way, the front door slamming open, 2
his cap on the floor, and the voice suddenly become raucous
shouting, "Isn't anybody *here*?"

At lunch he spoke insolently to his father, spilled his baby 3
sister's milk, and remarked that his teacher said we were not to
take the name of the Lord in vain.

"How *was* school today?" I asked, elaborately casual. 4

"All right," he said. 5

"Did you learn anything?" his father asked. 6

Laurie regarded his father coldly. "I didn't learn nothing," he 7
said.

"Anything," I said. "Didn't learn anything." 8

"The teacher spanked a boy, though," Laurie said, address- 9
ing his bread and butter. "For being fresh," he added, with his
mouth full.

"What did he do?" I asked. "Who was it?" 10

Laurie thought. "It was Charles," he said. "He was fresh. The 11
teacher spanked him and made him stand in a corner. He was
awfully fresh."

"What did he do?" I asked again, but Laurie slid off his chair, 12
took a cookie, and left, while his father was still saying, "See
here, young man."

The next day Laurie remarked at lunch, as soon as he sat 13
down, "Well, Charles was bad again today." He grinned enormously and said, "Today Charles hit the teacher."

"Good heavens," I said, mindful of the Lord's name, "I sup- 14
pose he got spanked again?"

"He sure did," Laurie said. "Look up," he said to his father. 15
"What?" his father said, looking up.

"Look down," Laurie said. "Look at my thumb. Gee, you're 16
dumb." He began to laugh insanely. 17

"Why did Charles hit the teacher?" I asked quickly. 18

"Because she tried to make him color with red crayons," 19
Laurie said. "Charles wanted to color with green crayons so he
hit the teacher and she spanked him and said nobody play with
Charles but everybody did."

The third day—it was Wednesday of the first week—Charles 20
bounced a see-saw onto the head of a little girl and made her
bleed, and the teacher made him stay inside all during recess.
Thursday Charles had to stand in a corner during story-time
because he kept pounding his feet on the floor. Friday Charles
was deprived of blackboard privileges because he threw chalk.

On Saturday I remarked to my husband, "Do you think 21
kindergarten is too unsettling for Laurie? All this toughness,
and bad grammar, and this Charles boy sounds like such a bad
influence."

"It'll be all right," my husband said reassuringly. "Bound to 22
be people like Charles in the world. Might as well meet them
now as later."

On Monday Laurie came home late, full of news. "Charles," 23
he shouted as he came up the hill; I was waiting anxiously on
the front steps. "Charles," Laurie yelled all the way up the hill,
"Charles was bad again."

"Come right in," I said, as soon as he came close enough. 24
"Lunch is waiting."

"You know what Charles did?" he demanded, following me 25
through the door. "Charles yelled so in school they sent a boy in
from first grade to tell the teacher she had to make Charles keep

quiet, and so Charles had to stay after school. And so all the children stayed to watch him."

"What did he do?" I asked.   26

"He just sat there," Laurie said, climbing into his chair at the   27
table. "Hi, Pop, y'old dust mop."

"Charles had to stay after school today," I told my husband.   28
"Everyone stayed with him."

"What does this Charles look like?" my husband asked   29
Laurie. "What's his other name?"

"He's bigger than me," Laurie said. "And he doesn't have   30
any rubbers and he doesn't ever wear a jacket."

Monday night was the first Parent-Teachers meeting, and   31
only the fact that the baby had a cold kept me from going; I
wanted passionately to meet Charles's mother. On Tuesday Laurie
remarked suddenly, "Our teacher had a friend come to see
her in school today."

"Charles's mother?" my husband and I asked simultane-   32
ously.

"Naaah," Laurie said scornfully. "It was a man who came   33
and made us do exercises, we had to touch our toes. Look."
He climbed down from his chair and squatted down and
touched his toes. "Like this," he said. He got solemnly back into
his chair and said, picking up his fork, "Charles didn't even *do*
exercises."

"That's fine," I said heartily. "Didn't Charles want to do   34
exercises?"

"Naaah," Laurie said. "Charles was so fresh to the teacher's   35
friend he wasn't *let* do exercises."

"Fresh again?" I said.   36

"He kicked the teacher's friend," Laurie said. "The teacher's   37
friend told Charles to touch his toes like I just did and Charles
kicked him."

"What are they going to do about Charles, do you suppose?"   38
Laurie's father asked him.

Laurie shrugged elaborately. "Throw him out of school, I   39
guess," he said.

Wednesday and Thursday were routine; Charles yelled dur- 40
ing story hour and hit a boy in the stomach and made him cry.
On Friday Charles stayed after school again and so did all the
other children.

With the third week of kindergarten Charles was an institu- 41
tion in our family; the baby was being a Charles when she cried
all afternoon; Laurie did a Charles when he filled his wagon full
of mud and pulled it through the kitchen; even my husband,
when he caught his elbow in the telephone cord and pulled telephone, ashtray, and a bowl of flowers off the table, said, after the
first minute, "Looks like Charles."

During the third and fourth weeks it looked like a reforma- 42
tion in Charles; Laurie reported grimly at lunch on Thursday of
the third week, "Charles was so good today the teacher gave
him an apple."

"What?" I said, and my husband added warily, "You mean 43
Charles?"

"Charles," Laurie said. "He gave the crayons around and he 44
picked up the books afterward and the teacher said he was her
helper."

"What happened?" I asked incredulously. 45

"He was her helper, that's all," Laurie said, and shrugged. 46

"Can this be true, about Charles?" I asked my husband that 47
night. "Can something like this happen?"

"Wait and see," my husband said cynically. "When you've 48
got a Charles to deal with, this may mean he's only plotting."

He seemed to be wrong. For over a week Charles was the 49
teacher's helper; each day he handed things out and he picked
things up; no one had to stay after school.

"The P.T.A. meeting's next week again," I told my husband 50
one evening. "I'm going to find Charles's mother there."

"Ask her what happened to Charles," my husband said. "I'd 51
like to know."

"I'd like to know myself," I said. 52

On Friday of that week things were back to normal. "You 53
know what Charles did today?" Laurie demanded at the lunch

table, in a voice slightly awed. "He told a little girl to say a word and she said it and the teacher washed her mouth out with soap and Charles laughed."

"What word?" his father asked unwisely, and Laurie said, 54 "I'll have to whisper it to you, it's so bad." He got down off his chair and went around to his father. His father bent his head down and Laurie whispered joyfully. His father's eyes widened.

"Did Charles tell the little girl to say *that*?" he asked 55 respectfully.

"She said it *twice*," Laurie said. "Charles told her to say it 56 *twice*."

"What happened to Charles?" my husband asked. 57

"Nothing," Laurie said. "He was passing out the crayons." 58

Monday morning Charles abandoned the little girl and said 59 the evil word himself three or four times, getting his mouth washed out with soap each time. He also threw chalk.

My husband came to the door with me that evening as I set 60 out for the P.T.A. meeting. "Invite her over for a cup of tea after the meeting," he said. "I want to get a look at her."

"If only she's there," I said prayerfully. 61

"She'll be there," my husband said. "I don't see how they 62 could hold a P.T.A. meeting without Charles's mother."

At the meeting I sat restlessly, scanning each comfortable 63 matronly face, trying to determine which one hid the secret of Charles. None of them looked to me haggard enough. No one stood up in the meeting and apologized for the way her son had been acting. No one mentioned Charles.

After the meeting I identified and sought out Laurie's 64 kindergarten teacher. She had a plate with a cup of tea and a piece of chocolate cake; I had a plate with a cup of tea and a piece of marshmallow cake. We maneuvered up to one another cautiously, and smiled.

"I've been so anxious to meet you," I said. "I'm Laurie's 65 mother."

"We're all so interested in Laurie," she said. 66

"Well, he certainly likes kindergarten," I said. "He talks about it all the time." 67

"We had a little trouble adjusting, the first week or so," she said primly, "but now he's a fine little helper. With occasional lapses, of course." 68

"Laurie usually adjusts very quickly," I said. "I suppose this time it's Charles's influence." 69

"Charles?" 70

"Yes," I said laughing, "you must have your hands full in that kindergarten, with Charles." 71

"Charles?" she said. "We don't have any Charles in the kindergarten." 72

 Focusing on the Story

1   Describe Laurie's behavior at home. How is it similar to Charles's behavior at school?

2   How does Laurie explain why he is late on Monday? Why is he really late?

3   Laurie's mother worries that "kindergarten is unsettling for Laurie." Why does she worry about Charles's behavior?

4   What is Laurie's attitude toward Charles? What does he think will happen to Charles?

5   Who is Laurie's mother looking for at the P.T.A. meeting? Does she find her? Who is Charles?

 Interpreting and Evaluating

1   Why does Laurie make up stories about Charles? Is he a disturbed child who needs psychiatric treatment? How should the parents handle Laurie's behavior? Should he be punished for lying? What would you have done if Laurie had been your child?

2   Why is the title of the story "Charles" when the story is really about Laurie? Would another title such as "Laurie" be better? Why or why not?

3   Author Shirley Jackson has sprinkled many clues throughout the story as to who Charles really is. At what point in the story did you suspect Charles's identity?

4   Although author Shirley Jackson doesn't describe Laurie's personality directly, she shows it through Laurie's words and actions. What can you infer about the kind of child Laurie is?

5   How do you think Laurie's mother feels when the teacher tells her that there is no Charles in kindergarten? How would you have felt if you had been Laurie's mother?

 Ideas for Writing and Further Discussion

1   Write a few paragraphs about a person you know well, such as a relative or a friend. Start with an overall impression of the person, and then instead of telling the reader what the person is like, show his or her personality through dialogue and action.

2   Write a narrative essay about a time when you blamed someone else for something you did. What did you do? Who did you blame, and what was the result?

It's not necessary to write a formal thesis statement in a narrative essay, but you may wish to start with a general statement that introduces the event and expresses an attitude toward the experience.

3   Write a narrative essay about an amusing childhood experience. Describe what happened. Did it end well or in disaster?

4   Write a narrative essay about an amusing experience you as an adult had with a child. The child may have been your own child, a younger sibling or someone else's child. Describe what happened. How did it end?

 An Additional Idea for Discussion and Writing

Discuss or write an essay in which you compare and/or contrast the writer in "A Mother in Mannville" by Marjorie Rawlings, Señora Ines in "The Stolen Party" by Liliana Heker, and the mother in "Charles" by Shirley Jackson. The end result will probably be a profile or a broad character sketch of three women who are far less perceptive than they think they are.

Suggested *thesis*: several ways in which they are similar or different.

Each *body paragraph* should explore one difference or similarity supported by examples from the stories.

Men and Women

Love and Relationships

The Answer Is No

Naguib Mahfouz

About the Author

Naguib Mahfouz is a well-known Egyptian author whose portrayal of life in present-day Egypt won him the Nobel Prize for Literature in 1988. His latest novel, *The Beginning and the End,* looks at the harsh life of ordinary Egyptians and in particular the plight of women. In addition to writing fiction, Naguib Mahfouz works as a journalist for the Egyptian newspaper *Al Ahram.*

 Something to Think About

In some Third-World countries such as Egypt, the setting of the following story, a woman loses her prospects for marriage if she loses her virginity, even if she is raped. What do you think might be a woman's options if she finds herself in such a situation?

 Words to Keep in Mind

headmaster *(1)* principal

decorously *(4)* politely; showing good taste in behavior, speech, and dress

attired *(4)* dressed

spherical *(4)* round

attained *(11)* achieved, gained

byword *(12)* one that is proverbial as a type of specified characteristics

rapacious *(12)* greedy

coercion *(13)* force

solitude *(13)* being alone

asperity *(14)* harshness or sharpness of temper

T he important piece of news that the new headmaster   1
had arrived spread through the school. She heard of it in
the women teachers' common room as she was casting a final
glance at the day's lessons. There was no getting away from join-
ing the other teachers in congratulating him, and from shaking
him by the hand too. A shudder passed through her body, but it
was unavoidable.

"They speak highly of his ability," said a colleague of hers.   2
"And they talk too of his strictness."

It had always been a possibility that might occur, and now it   3
had. Her pretty face paled, and a staring look came to her wide
black eyes.

When the time came, the teachers went in single file, deco-   4
rously attired, to his open room. He stood behind his desk as he
received the men and women. He was of medium height, with a
tendency to portliness, and had a spherical face, hooked nose,
and bulging eyes; the first thing that could be seen of him was a
thick, puffed-up mustache, arched like a foam-laden wave. She
advanced with her eyes fixed on his chest. Avoiding his gaze,
she stretched out her hand. What was she to say? Just what the
others had said? However, she kept silent, uttered not a word.
What, she wondered, did his eyes express? His rough hand
shook hers, and he said in a gruff voice, "Thanks." She turned
elegantly and moved off.

She forgot her worries through her daily tasks, though she   5
did not look in good shape. Several of the girls remarked, "Miss
is in a bad mood." When she returned to her home at the beginning of the Pyramids Road, she changed her clothes and sat
down to eat with her mother. "Everything all right?" inquired
her mother, looking her in the face.

"Badran, Badran Badawi," she said briefly. "Do you remem-   6
ber him? He's been appointed our headmaster."

From *The Time and the Place and Other Stories* by Naguib Mahfouz. Translated
by Denys Johnson-Davies. © 1991 by the American University in Cairo
Press. Used by permission of Doubleday, a division of Random House,
Inc.

"Really!"

Then, after a moment of silence, she said, "It's of no importance at all—it's an old and long-forgotten story."

After eating, she took herself off to her study to rest for a
while before correcting some exercise books. She had forgotten
him completely. No, not completely. How could he be forgotten
completely? When he had first come to give her a private lesson
in mathematics, she was fourteen years of age. In fact not quite
fourteen. He had been twenty-five years older, the same age as
her father. She had said to her mother, "His appearance is a
mess, but he explains things well." And her mother had said,
"We're not concerned with what he looks like; what's important
is how he explains things."

He was an amusing person, and she got on well with him
and benefited from his knowledge. How, then, had it happened?
In her innocence she had not noticed any change in his behavior
to put her on her guard. Then one day he had been left on his
own with her, her father having gone to her aunt's clinic. She
had not the slightest doubts about a man she regarded as a second father. How, then, had it happened? Without love or desire
on her part the thing had happened. She had asked in terror
about what had occurred, and he had told her, "Don't be frightened or sad. Keep it to yourself and I'll come and propose to you
the day you come of age."

And he had kept his promise and had come to ask for her
hand. By then she had attained a degree of maturity that gave
her an understanding of the dimensions of her tragic position.
She had found that she had no love or respect for him and that
he was as far as he could be from her dreams and from the ideas
she had formed of what constituted an ideal and moral person.
But what was to be done? Her father had passed away two years
ago, and her mother had been taken aback by the forwardness of
the man. However, she had said to her, "I know your attachment
to your personal independence, so I leave the decision to you."

She had been conscious of the critical position she was
in. She had either to accept or to close the door forever. It was
the sort of situation that could force her into something she
detested. She was the rich, beautiful girl, a byword in Abbasiyya

for her nobility of character, and now here she was struggling helplessly in a well-sprung trap, while he looked down at her with rapacious eyes. Just as she had hated his strength, so too did she hate her own weakness. To have abused her innocence was one thing, but for him to have the upper hand now that she was fully in possession of her faculties was something else. He had said, "So here I am, making good my promise because I love you." He had also said, "I know of your love of teaching, and you will complete your studies at the College of Science."

She had felt such anger as she had never felt before. She had 13 rejected coercion in the same way as she rejected ugliness. It had meant little to her to sacrifice marriage. She had welcomed being on her own, for solitude accompanied by self-respect was not loneliness. She had also guessed he was after her money. She had told her mother quite straightforwardly, "No," to which her mother had replied, "I am astonished you did not make this decision from the first moment."

The man had blocked her way outside and said, "How can 14 you refuse? Don't you realize the outcome?" And she had replied with an asperity he had not expected, "For me any out- come is preferable to being married to you."

After finishing her studies, she had wanted something to do 15 to fill her spare time, so she had worked as a teacher. Chances to marry had come time after time, but she had turned her back on them all.

"Does no one please you?" her mother asked her. 16
"I know what I'm doing," she had said gently. 17
"But time is going by." 18
"Let it go as it pleases, I am content." 19

Day by day she becomes older. She avoids love, fears it. With 20 all her strength she hopes that life will pass calmly, peacefully, rather than happily. She goes on persuading herself that happi- ness is not confined to love and motherhood. Never has she regretted her firm decision. Who knows what the morrow holds? But she was certainly unhappy that he should again make his appearance in her life, that she would be dealing with him day after day, and that he would be making of the past a living and painful present.

Then, the first time he was alone with her in his room, he 21
asked her, "How are you?"

She answered coldly, "I'm fine." 22

He hesitated slightly before inquiring, "Have you not . . . I 23
mean, did you get married?"

In the tone of someone intent on cutting short a conversa- 24
tion, she said, "I told you, I'm fine."

 Focusing on the Story

1   Describe the main character. Is she attractive and educated? What is her economic status?

2   From where does the main character know the new headmaster, Badran Badawi? What had their relationship been?

3   What crime had been committed against the main character when she was about fourteen? Why didn't she tell her parents about the incident? Did she report it to the police?

4   Why is the main character's mother astonished that the daughter takes so long to refuse the old tutor's marriage proposal? Similarly, why is she at a loss when her daughter refuses other marriage proposals?

 Interpreting and Evaluating

1   The author, Naguib Mahfouz, has not given the main character a name. What may be some reasons for this omission?

2   After the main character has made her decision not to marry her old tutor, the tutor asks incredulously, "How can you refuse? Don't you realize the outcome?" What does the old tutor mean? Considering that in the Moslem culture a woman loses her opportunity for marriage when she loses her virginity, do you think it is a difficult decision for the main character? Explain.

3   Why does the main character avoid and fear love? Is her fear necessarily based on cultural restrictions alone?

4   Why is rape a particularly heinous crime? What are some emotional scars that rape may leave?

5   To what does the title "The Answer Is No" refer? Give examples of several "no's" in the answer.

6   The main character tries to persuade herself that "happiness is not confined to love and motherhood." Is a woman's happiness confined to love and motherhood, in your opinion? Explain.

 Ideas for Writing and Further Discussion

1   Why do some men commit crimes specifically against women? What, if anything, in their background and personality could account for such acts? Write an essay in which you explore reasons why men commit such crimes.

Suggested *thesis*: two or three such reasons.

Each *body paragraph* should discuss one reason.

2   What are some career options women have today that were not available to our mothers and grandmothers? Write an essay in which you compare and contrast the choices available to our mothers and grandmothers with the choices women have today.

Suggested *thesis*: several areas that are open to women today that were not open to our mothers and grandmothers.

Each *body paragraph* might compare and contrast one area. Or, one body paragraph might deal with the few areas open to our mothers and grandmothers. Two other body paragraphs might then deal with two different areas open to women today.

Butterfly Man

The Maidu Indians
(recorded by Dr. Roland Dixon)

About the Authors

The Maidu Indians made their home in northeastern California between the Sacramento River and the Sierras. Dr. Roland Dixon made several trips to study the Maidu and recorded many of their stories. "Butterfly Man" was recorded sometime around 1900.

 Something to Think About

What will happen to a woman who leaves her baby to run after butterflies that turn out to be beautiful men in disguise?

 Words to Keep in Mind

tabu *(1)* something forbidden by tradition (taboo)
cradleboard *(2)* used by Native American women to transport babies
manzanita *(4)* evergreen shrub common in northeastern California
dentalium shell *(10)* tooth shell
abalone shell *(10)* pretty shell, slightly spiral in form and lined with mother-of-pearl

I t was springtime along the river and Tolowim-Woman was restless and lonely. Tolowim-Man was downriver spearing salmon. She knew that when he came home, he would join the other men in the sweat house. This was the time of the spring deer drive, the time when a woman is unclean and is avoided by her husband if he is taking part in the drive. Tolowim-Man must keep himself absolutely pure now for he was one of those who would impersonate the deer, and this is a dangerous thing to do at best. This was the time for a good wife to stay indoors and to help to see that no tabu was broken.

Tolowim-Woman was a good wife, but she remembered that 2 spring is also the time when wild iris blooms in the hills. And Tolowim-Woman was weary of women's gossip and women's voices. So, she settled her basket hat straight on her head and let herself quietly out of her house by way of the low front passage. She took care not to jiggle or disturb the baby on his cradleboard at her back.

Once outside she stood erect, gazed briefly up and down the 3 river, then turned away from it and walked up into the hills.

The sun was bright and hot. After walking for some time 4 Tolowim-Woman, out of breath, slipped the carrying strap from her forehead and put the cradleboard in the shade of a man-zanita bush and sat down to rest.

As she sat, a butterfly fluttered softly by. It brushed the 5 baby's arm, causing him to laugh and try to touch it.

It brushed Tolowim-Woman's cheek and she too laughed 6 and tried to touch it. It settled for a moment on a branch of the manzanita bush, and Tolowim-Woman, laughing again, stretched quickly forward to cover it with her seed basket. But it fluttered on to the next bush, just out of her reach. She got up from the ground, following and trying to capture it.

She wanted this butterfly as she had not wanted anything for 7 a long, long time. It was large and strong-flying as butterflies rarely are, and it was very beautiful, with wing bands black as the mussel's shell and stripes scarlet as the woodpecker's crest.

The butterfly was so little ahead of her that each new step or 8 reach seemed to be the one that would capture it. But always it kept its free fluttering way, just ahead, just out of reach. Nor was it flying at random, for its start-and-stop course was leading her ever up and back, farther into the hills, farther from the river.

Tolowim-Woman looked back at the baby, sleepy and com- 9
fortable in the shade of the manzanita bush. She had come a long
way from him. The butterfly would tire soon now. She would
make a last try for it over this next hill and take it back to the
baby.

But the butterfly did not tire nor did it allow itself to be cap- 10
tured. Tolowim-Woman became so intent on possessing it that
through the long afternoon it led her on and on. Her buckskin
skirt was dirty and torn from the thorny bushes. Her cap was
brushed from her head, and she did not stop to pick it up. And
the heavy strings of polished dentalium and abalone shell about
her neck were broken, scattered and lost.

At last as the sun was setting, and far inland, among hills she 11
did not know, Tolowim-Woman sank exhausted to the ground.
The butterfly turned at once, and fluttered back to her. It came
and settled down beside her. In the dusk she saw that it was
become a swift and graceful man, naked save for the butterfly
girdle encircling his waist, his long hair held in a black and red
headband.

Together they passed the night, Tolowim-Woman and But- 12
terfly Man. In the morning, Butterfly Man asked her, "You wish
to go with me?"

She answered, "Yes! I do." 13

Then he said to her, "That is good. One more day's travelling 14
will bring us to my land, and there we shall live. But it is a long
and dangerous way, O my Wife. We must cross the Valley of Butterflies and they will try to take you from me. Will you do as I
say that I may lead you safely through?"

She promised to do as he told her. He said, "Follow close 15
behind me. Step where I step. Hold tight with both your hands
to my girdle. Do not let go even for a moment. And do not look
at any butterfly until we are out of the valley. Obey me for this
time and you shall be forever safe. Remember, I lose my power
to protect you if you haven't your hands on my girdle."

They started off, Butterfly Man in the lead, Tolowim-Woman 16
following. She grasped the girdle firmly in both her hands and

she looked only at the ground. In this manner they came to the Valley of Butterflies and travelled some distance into it.

It was rough underfoot and Butterfly Man set a straight, fast course—down, across, up. 17

Butterflies hovered on the rocks over which they had to step. 18 Butterflies caught against their legs and in their hair and fluttered before their faces. The air of the valley seemed to be entirely filled with butterflies.

For a long time Tolowim-Woman remembered to keep her 19 hands on the girdle and her eyes on the pathless way underfoot. But then a butterfly, all black, larger even than Butterfly Man had been, and shining as the crow, hovered before her. He hovered just above her breasts in the line of her downcast eyes and settled for a long moment on her lips. Then he flew slowly away. She gasped with the excitement of his beauty. Her eyes followed his flight and she took one hand off the girdle and reached greedily for him.

He was gone. 20

But at once a hundred, a thousand others danced before her, 21 against her eyes and cheeks and mouth. They were black and pure white and pale gold and swamp green and iris purple.

She wanted them all, and she let go her hold on Butterfly 22 Man's girdle and reached for them with both her hands.

Not one could she catch. 23

Butterfly Man did not stop or look back. She kept him in 24 sight for a time, but as she clutched ever more wildly at one and then another, she fell far, far behind him.

She ran after this butterfly and that one, here and there, up 25 and down, stumbling, desperate, at random, always reaching for another one and always missing it.

Her hair was unbraided and tangled, her skirt kept catching 26 in the bushes and holding her back. She untied it and threw it away. Her moccasins were in shreds. Naked except for her bark apron, dishevelled, obsessed, she continued her hopeless chase.

Butterfly Man was gone now. He was across the valley and 27 in his own land.

Tolowim-Woman followed one butterfly and then another, 28
on and on and on. And then her heart went away, and this was
the end of Tolowim-Woman.

 Focusing on the Story

1   When must Tolowim-Man stay away from his wife according to
this story?

2   What are some important sources of food for the Tolowim Indian
tribe, an imaginary tribe made up by the Maidu Indians?

3   Describe Tolowim-Woman as she is leaving her house and walking
into the hills. What is she wearing? What does she take with her?

4   With whom does Tolowim-Woman spend the night in the hills?
What does her companion tell her to do so that he "may lead [her]
safely through" the Valley of Butterflies?

5   What happens when a shiny black butterfly hovers "just above her
breasts in the line of her downcast eyes"? Does Tolowim-Woman catch
him? Does she catch any of the other butterflies? What happens to
Tolowim-Woman in the end?

 Interpreting and Evaluating

1   Why does Tolowim-Woman decide to leave her house and go into
the hills? Why does she become so obsessed with the butterflies?

2   What might the butterflies represent? Give evidence from the story
to support your opinion. How is the ending inevitable?

3   Tolowim-Woman leaves her baby under a bush to chase the butterflies. What does this action say about her sense of responsibility?
What other inferences can you make about her character from the
story?

4   If this is a morality tale, a cautionary tale, or a fable, what is the
moral of the story?

5   The story was told by the Maidu Indians, but the events in the
story occur among the imaginary Tolowim tribe outside the Maidu
world. What may be the reason for having the characters be outsiders?

Ideas for Writing and Further Discussion

1   The Butterfly Man may have been the product of a woman's day-dreaming. What evidence can you find in the story for such an interpretation? What in Indian lore may lend support to the fact that this story is a woman's fantasy? For example, the Indian women had to spend much time alone. Furthermore, it was the women who gathered berries, fruit, and nuts in the California hills, which are often alive with colorful butterflies. Finally, what traits does a butterfly possess that may fuel a woman's fantasy of a beautiful man in disguise?

Write an essay in which you discuss several reasons why the story "Butterfly Man" may be bedded in a woman's imagination. Use the above suggestions as well as others of your own to develop your essay.

Suggested *thesis*: two or three reasons why "Butterfly Man" may be a product of a woman's fantasy.

Each *body paragraph* should provide supporting details for one such reason.

2   The grass is always greener on the other side of the fence, according to an old saying. Have you ever tried to go after something that you didn't have at the expense of something that you already had?

Write a paragraph or two about a time when you sacrificed something you had for something you desired. Describe what happened. What was the outcome? Did you learn anything from the experience?

The Cock

Tao Kim Hai

About the Author

Tao Kim Hai, a Vietnamese journalist and short story writer, is known in French literary circles. Tao Kim Hai has written several books on former French Indo-China.

 Something to Think About

Do you have a favorite possession that has a special meaning just to you? Why is it special?

 Words to Keep in Mind

betel *(1)* a pepper tree whose leaves are chewed with lime and betel nut as a stimulant in Southeast Asia

conjugal *(2)* related to the sexual aspect of marriage

crop *(2)* wide part of the throat or neck of a bird

deposed *(2)* removed from a throne or other high position

spurs *(2)* sharp spines on the foot of a game cock used for slashing his opponent

monochord *(4)* instrument with one string

paddy *(6)* rice in the husk

trysting-place *(8)* lovers' secret meeting place

lethal *(12)* deadly

saber *(12)* sword

palaver *(14)* long discussion

tête-a-tête *(14)* intimate meeting

prostrate *(14)* to lie face down in submission or adoration

barge *(16)* flat-bottomed boat usually towed

piastres *(16)* unit of currency in former South Vietnam

Y ou're quite right; he has certainly outlived his useful- 1
ness, and we should kill him. But my husband would
never agree to it, and neither would I. Help yourself to betel
again, honored sister, and I will tell you why.

Yes, he's getting quite old for a rooster, and he doesn't per- 2
form his conjugal duties as he should. But there's no question of
killing him, nor even of giving his harem to a younger cock. In
the first place, he'd fight until his crop was torn open rather than
be deposed. He comes of fighting stock—see how long and
sharp his spurs are, and how they curve. And in spite of his age,
he's still fast enough on his feet to defend his rights. His feet are
his most aristocratic feature; notice how the scales grow in two
straight lines like the Chinese mottoes on either side of a door,
with not a sign of a feather between them. His mother was only
an ordinary Cochin-China hen, but his sire was a real Cambo-
dian fighting cock with I've no idea how many fights to his
credit. But that's neither here nor there; it's not for his fighting
blood that I value him. The truth is that he did me a great service
five years ago. It's thanks to my poor old rooster that I married
the man I love.

Five years ago, my husband lived next door to my parents. 3
We were neighbors, but the distance between us was immeasur-
able, unbridgeable. He had neither father nor mother; my father
was the *ly-truong* (mayor) of the community. His house was a
little hut built on date-palm posts, walled with bamboo and
thatched with water-palm leaves; my house had four rows of
carved teakwood columns, walls of whitewashed brick and a
red-tiled roof. My father had twenty oxen and ten buffaloes, and

---

From *Asia Magazine,* March 1946. United Nations World. Translated by Ruth
Barber.

a thousand acres of rice fields; *he* hadn't even a patch of ground, and raised only a few chickens. To tell the truth, he was our *ta-diên* (tenant farmer).

Tenant or no, he was the handsomest young man, the best 4 monochord player and the fastest rice planter of the whole district. You should have heard him play the monochord in those days; it was enough to bring a goddess down from heaven. I've made him give up playing since we've been married, although I love music myself. It wasn't all because I was jealous of his monochord; I was afraid for his eyesight, too. Everybody says the monochord causes blindness, and the better the musician, the greater the danger.

He was eighteen, and I was two years younger. We were in 5 love, and our love was all the stronger because it was hopeless. An irresistible attraction drew me to him, in spite of his rough farm clothes and his unkempt hair.

In his poultry yard a young cock with green and gold 6 plumage and a blood-red comb lorded it over the admiring hens. He fought all the other cocks in the village, and gallantly refused the paddy and broken rice thrown to his little flock until his wives had eaten their fill. He was brave, and he was not at all bashful, either with the hens or before me. You would have said he took a wicked delight in making love to them in my presence. Then he would cock a glittering eye at me, and crow.

One day his master and I were talking behind the bamboo 7 hut, where we were safe from all indiscreet eyes. Suddenly we heard a loud "Ha, ha, ha!" We turned around in alarm; it was only the cock. My suitor threw a stick at him. He saw it coming and made a magnificent leap to one side, so that the stick only grazed his tail. Then with an indignant "Kut-kut-kut" he stalked off to rejoin his hens, looking for all the world like an insulted sovereign. From the safety of the poultry yard he looked back at us, and, like a practical joker who has just pulled off a good one, he crowed, "Ha, ha, ha, ha-a-a-!"

Another day we had found a trysting-place at the foot of a 8 big straw-stack, from which we could look out over the endless reaches of my father's rice fields, the obstacle to our marriage.

That accursed cock came and perched on top of the straw-stack, discovered us and, beating his wings in the air as if to call the whole world to witness, he let out a scandalized "Oh-oh-oh-rooo!"

In trying to chase the old tattle-tale away, we lost all sense of 9
caution, and he was not the only one to see us together that time. Soon the village was buzzing with gossip about us; the cock had set tongues wagging. Jealous girls, and young men too, whispered that I had lost my virtue, and the old *bagia* shook their heads and began to speculate on the date when my figure would show the results of my fall. And of course the rumors did not fail to reach my parents' ears.

The cock joined the other gossips. No longer satisfied to 10
crow all day, he started to crow in the evening, too, after the lamps were lit. His competitors, a thousand times outcrowed but still ambitious, replied from all the henhouses of the village. You never heard such a racket.

Do you believe here in your province, honorable elder sister, 11
that the crowing of a cock in the evening is the sign of an extra-marital pregnancy? In our district everybody believed it, even my mother. My poor mother is superstitious. In spite of my tears and my denials, she took me for a lost virgin who dared not acknowledge her fall. No need for *me* to admit it; the cocks were there to proclaim it far and wide.

My grandparents were summoned, and my aunts and uncles 12
on my mother's side and on my father's. They shut me up in my little room and held a family caucus in the living room before the altar of our ancestors. I thought my last hour was come, and I waited for them to bring me the lethal cup, the saber and the red silk cord. Which death should I choose—poisoning, bleeding or hanging? Would they shave my head like a nun's before they forced me to commit suicide? Suicide it certainly must be, for the family of a mayor must never lose face.

But I was an only child, and my mother was already old. No 13
matter what the sacrifice, the family must have another genera-tion to carry on the cult of the ancestors. If I were to die without issue, my mother would be forced to choose a concubine for my

father and to admit her to the marriage bed, to cherish the concubine's children as her own. Then, too, I suspect that my father was beginning to be influenced by European ideas. Above all, he loved me a great deal, although the traditional reserve that a father must observe toward his daughter kept him from showing it. Whatever the reason, the family council decided to do nothing worse than to marry me off in all haste. And to whom, God in Heaven? To my seducer, no less. I agreed without a murmur.

The six preliminary marriage ceremonies were gotten   14
through with before two weeks had passed, and we were married in the strictest privacy. The formal proposal was without pomp and palaver; the betel ceremony was reduced to little more than a tête-a-tête in everyday clothes. As for the suitor's period of probation in the house of his future wife, which usually lasts from six months to two years, we simply omitted it. No invitations on scarlet paper with gold script, no official delegation from the town council, no gift of ring-necked ducks on a brass platter, no open-air banquet lasting far into the night. But there were also none of those more or less annoying jokes which most young couples have to resign themselves to—the drinking party in the bridal chamber, the bed that rocks, the bridegroom who is kidnapped. We had only to prostrate ourselves, I in a wide-sleeved red dress and he in a black tunic and turban, before the altars of our ancestors and before my parents, less to ask their benediction than to make honorable amends.

It was a bad match, and a scandalous one; the less said the   15
better.

It had been agreed that we should leave our native village   16
immediately and make our home in some distant province where we were not known. On our wedding night we set out on the long journey, in a big barge that my parents had loaded with rice, salt fish, and *piastres*. We were accompanied by two faithful servants and the cock, who followed us into exile with all his little harem.

We've been here for five years now, honorable sister, in your   17
rich and peaceful province, and as you know, we haven't yet had a child. My poor mother writes me that she spends her days run-

ning to the pagodas having prayers said and sacrifices made, in the hope of becoming a grandmother before she goes to join her ancestors at the Golden Spring. The poor old cock has been proved a liar. But thanks to his lies I'm a happy woman, and he shall have all the white rice he can eat to the end of his days.

 Focusing on the Story

1   Where is the narrator (the character who tells the story), and to whom is she talking?

2   Why is the rooster so special to the narrator? What does it symbolize?

3   Why was the narrator attracted to the young man? What were the basic obstacles to their marriage?

4   When the family discovered the secret relationship between the narrator and her boyfriend, the relatives were summoned, and they "held a family caucus in the living room before the altar of [the] ancestors." What was often expected of a daughter who disgraced the family in this or any other way? What awful choices would the narrator have had if her family had brought her "the lethal cup, the saber, and the red silk cord"?

5   There are hints of several superstitious beliefs in the story. Name at least two.

 Interpreting and Evaluating

1   Why was the narrator allowed to marry her suitor after all? Why did the newlyweds have to leave the village? Is the narrator happy? Are the parents happy? Give evidence from the story to support your opinion.

2   Did the narrator's parents do the right thing by sending their daughter and son-in-law away? Should they have been less influenced by the social pressure of the town in which they lived? How can tradition and social pressure be both good and bad?

3   If the narrator had married someone of her own status, elaborate ceremonies would have been planned. Did the narrator miss out on a great party, or did she escape a dreadful ordeal?

4   Although the setting is Vietnam, the basic story plot (what's happening in the story) is similar to many Western stories. What other stories have you read or seen on television or in the movies that have similar story lines or plots?

5   Even under the most ideal circumstances, marriage can be a difficult undertaking. How can marriage become even more difficult if the partners are from different backgrounds? How can these difficulties be overcome?

 Ideas for Writing and Further Discussion

1   Do you have a favorite possession with a special symbolic significance? Write a paragraph describing such a possession, and explain why it is special. Begin with a general sentence that expresses your attitude toward the object.

2   As the saying goes, forbidden fruit tastes sweetest. If you agree, take a stand and write an essay in which you give examples from your own experience that prove this saying to be true.

Suggested *thesis*: two or three examples that support your stand.

Each *body paragraph* should look at one example and show how it proves the above saying to be true.

3   Are you superstitious? Do you knock on wood? Do you avoid walking under a ladder? Why do you think people are superstitious? Write an essay in which you describe some common superstitions that people you know believe in.

Suggested *thesis*: two or three such superstitions.

Each *body paragraph* should describe one superstition and explain why people believe in it and how it affects them.

Difficulty
with a Bouquet

William Sansom

About the Author

William Sansom was a British writer who wrote about life in his native London. He died in 1976.

 Something to Think About

When was the last time you did something nice for a fellow human without expecting anything in return? Why are we suspicious of people who want to give us gifts for no apparent reason? What has happened to simple brotherhood (or sisterhood) in our fast-paced society?

 Words to Keep in Mind

chestnuts *(2)* trees with large leaves

hollyhocks *(2)* tall plants with large flowers of various colors

ulterior *(6)* hidden

affectation *(6)* artificial behavior intended to impress others

aggrandizement *(7)* increase in power or wealth

seduction *(7)* tempting someone to do something wrong, especially sexually

motive *(7)* an inner drive or impulse that causes a person to act in a certain way

flinched *(8)* drew back as a show of weakness; winced

bravados *(8)* pretended couragous acts

maudlin *(11)* sentimental

S eal, walking through his garden, said suddenly to him- 1
self: "I would like to pick some flowers and take them to
Miss D."

The afternoon was light and warm. Tall chestnuts fanned 2
themselves in a pleasant breeze. Among the hollyhocks there
was a good humming as the bees tumbled from flower to flower.
Seal wore an open shirt. He felt fresh and fine, with the air swimming coolly under his shirt and around his ribs. The summer's
afternoon was free. Nothing pressed him. It was a time when
some simple, disinterested impulse might well be hoped to
flourish.

Seal felt a great joy in the flowers around him and from this a 3
brilliant longing to give. He wished to give quite inside himself,
uncritically, without thinking for a moment: "Here am I, Seal,
wishing something." Seal merely wanted to give some of his
flowers to a fellow being. It had happened that Miss D was the
first person to come to mind. He was in no way attached to Miss
D. He knew her slightly, as a plain, elderly girl of about twenty
who had come to live in the flats opposite his garden. If Seal had
ever thought about Miss D at all, it was because he disliked the
way she walked. She walked stiffly, sailing with her long body
while her little legs raced to catch up with it. But he was not
thinking of this now. Just by chance he had glimpsed the block
of flats as he had stooped to pick a flower. The flats had presented the image of Miss D to his mind.

Seal chose common, ordinary flowers. As the stems broke he 4
whistled between his teeth. He had chosen these ordinary flowers because they were the nearest to hand: in the second place,
because they were fresh and full of life. They were neither rare
nor costly. They were pleasant, fresh, unassuming flowers.

With the flowers in his hand, Seal walked contentedly from 5
his garden and set foot on the asphalt pavement that led to the

---

block of flats across the way. But as his foot touched the asphalt, as the sly glare of an old man fixed his eye for the moment of its passing, as the traffic asserted itself, certain misgivings began to freeze his impromptu joy. "Good heavens," he suddenly thought, "what am I doing?" He stepped outside himself and saw Seal carrying a bunch of cheap flowers to Miss D in the flats across the way.

"These are cheap flowers," he thought. "This is a sudden gift; I shall smile as I hand them to her. We shall both know that there is no ulterior reason for the gift and thus the whole action will smack of goodness—of goodness and simple brotherhood. And somehow . . . for that reason this gesture of mine will appear to be the most calculated pose of all. Such a simple gesture is improbable. The improbable is to be suspected. My gift will certainly be regarded as an affectation.

"Oh, if only I had some reason—aggrandizement, financial gain, seduction—any of the accepted motives that would return my flowers to social favor. But no—I have none of these in me. I only wish to give and to receive nothing in return."

As he walked on, Seal could see himself bowing and smiling. He saw himself smile too broadly as he apologized by exaggeration for his good action. His neck flinched with disgust as he saw himself assume the old bravados. He could see the mocking smile of recognition on the face of Miss D.

Seal dropped the flowers into the gutter and walked slowly back to his garden.

From her window high up in the concrete flats, Miss D watched Seal drop the flowers. How fresh they looked! How they would have livened her barren room! "Wouldn't it have been nice," thought Miss D, "if that Mr. Seal had been bringing *me* that pretty bouquet of flowers! Wouldn't it have been nice if he had picked them in his own garden and—well, just brought them along, quite casually, and made me a present of the delightful afternoon." Miss D dreamed on for a few minutes.

Then she frowned, rose, straightened her suspender belt, hurried into the kitchen. "Thank God he didn't," she sighed to herself. "I should have been most embarrassed. It's not as if he wanted me. It would have been just too maudlin for words."

Focusing on the Story

1   Describe Miss D. Is she attractive? Where does she live? How would you describe her lifestyle?

2   How would you describe Seal's relationship with Miss D? Is he in love with her?

3   What are some of Seal's thoughts as he steps "outside himself and [sees himself] carrying a bunch of cheap flowers to Miss D in the flats across the way"?

4   What are Miss D's first thoughts when she sees Seal drop the flowers in the gutter?

 Interpreting and Evaluating

1   Why does Seal want to give flowers to Miss D? Why do "common, ordinary flowers" seem appropriate?

2   Why does Seal think his gift will be "regarded as an affectation," and why will his friendly gesture seem calculated and suspicious?

3   After watching Seal drop the flowers, Miss D "frowned, rose, straightened her suspender belt, hurried into the kitchen. 'Thank God he didn't,' she sighed to herself. 'I should have been most embarrassed.'" Why would she have been embarrassed if Seal had given her the flowers?

4   Irony is the difference between what is expected and what actually happens. What is ironic in this story?

5   What are some common occasions for giving gifts? Would any of them apply to Seal?

6   Seal says that his gift of flowers will "smack of goodness . . . and simple brotherhood," so he tosses the flowers in the gutter. Why is a simple good deed to be suspected today? Have we as a society lost something valuable? Explain.

 Idea for Writing or Further Discussion

What kinds of gifts do you like to give? When do you like to give gifts? Write about different occasions when you give presents in your family. Give examples of gifts that are appropriate for each occasion.

Suggested *thesis*: three or four of your favorite occasions for giving gifts.

Each *body paragraph* should discuss one such occasion and give examples of gifts appropriate for that occasion.

The Gift of the Magi

O. Henry

About the Author

O. Henry, a pseudonym for William Sydney Porter, was an American short story writer whose stories depict life in New York during the first decade of the twentieth century. Many of O. Henry's stories have been translated into dozens of languages.

 Something to Think About

It's been said that the best things in life are free. What does this mean?

 Words to Keep in Mind

magi *(title)* three wise men of the East who brought gifts for baby Jesus

imputation of parsimony *(1)* feeling that people think you are stingy

beggar *(3)* to seem inadequate

mendicancy squad *(3)* police squad charged with chasing away beggars

vestibule *(4)* hallway

appertaining *(4)* belonging

pier-glass *(7)* tall mirror set in a wall between windows

Queen of Sheba *(9)* queen from South Arabia known for her beauty

King Solomon *(9)* king of Israel famous for his wealth and wisdom

cascade *(10)* waterfall

hashed *(18)* spoiled by clumsy work

metaphor *(18)* figure of speech

fob *(19)* small chain attached to a pocket watch

chaste *(19)* pure, simple in design
meretricious *(19)* too showy or flashy
prudence *(20)* caution
quail *(26)* kind of game bird
enfolded *(34)* embraced, hugged
inconsequential *(34)* unimportant
assertion *(34)* statement
illuminated *(34)* explained
tresses *(38)* long locks of hair
coveted *(38)* longed for with envy

O ne dollar and eighty-seven cents. That was all. And 60 1 cents of it was in pennies. Pennies saved one and two at a time by bulldozing the grocer and the vegetable man and the butcher until one's cheeks burned with the silent imputation of parsimony that such close dealing implied. Three times Della counted it. One dollar and eighty-seven cents. And the next day would be Christmas.

There was clearly nothing to do but flop down on the shabby 2 little couch and howl. So Della did it. Which instigates the moral reflection that life is made up of sobs, sniffles and smiles, with sniffles predominating.

While the mistress of the home is gradually subsiding from 3 the first stage to the second take a look at the home. A furnished flat at $8 per week. It did not exactly beggar description, but it certainly had that word on the lookout for the mendicancy squad.

In the vestibule below belonged to this flat a letter-box into 4 which no letter would go, and an electric button from which no mortal finger could coax a ring. Also appertaining thereunto was a card bearing the name "Mr. James Dillingham Young."

First published in *New York Sunday World Magazine,* December 10, 1905.

The "Dillingham" had been flung to the breeze during a for- 5
mer period of prosperity when its possessor was being paid $30
per week. Now, when the income was shrunk to $20, the letters
of "Dillingham" looked blurred, as though they were thinking
seriously of contracting to a modest and unassuming D. But
whenever Mr. James Dillingham Young came home and reached
his flat above he was called "Jim" and greatly hugged by Mrs.
James Dillingham Young, already introduced to you as Della.
Which is all very good.

Della finished her cry and attended to her cheeks with the 6
powder rag. She stood by the window and looked out dully at a
gray cat walking a gray fence in a gray backyard. Tomorrow
would be Christmas Day, and she had only $1.87 with which to
buy Jim a present. She had been saving every penny she could
for months, with this result. Twenty dollars a week doesn't go
far. Expenses had been greater than she had calculated. They
always are. Only $1.87 to buy a present for Jim. Her Jim. Many a
happy hour she had spent planning for something nice for him.
Something fine and rare and sterling—something just a little bit
near to being worthy of the honor of being owned by Jim.

There was a pier-glass between the windows of the room. 7
Perhaps you have seen a pier-glass in an $8 flat. A very thin and
very agile person may, by observing his reflection in a rapid
sequence of longitudinal strips, obtain a fairly accurate concep-
tion of his looks. Della, being slender, had mastered the art.

Suddenly she whirled from the window and stood before the 8
glass. Her eyes were shining brilliantly, but her face had lost its
color within twenty seconds. Rapidly she pulled down her hair
and let it fall to its full length.

Now, there were two possessions of the James Dillingham 9
Youngs in which they both took a mighty pride. One was Jim's
gold watch that had been his father's and his grandfather's. The
other was Della's hair. Had the Queen of Sheba lived in the flat
across the airshaft Della would have let her hair hang out the
window some day to dry and mocked at Her Majesty's jewels
and gifts. Had King Solomon been the janitor, with all his treasures piled up in the basement, Jim would have pulled out his

watch every time he passed, just to see him pluck at his beard from envy.

So now Della's beautiful hair fell about her, rippling and shin- 10
ing like a cascade of brown waters. It reached below her knee and made itself almost a garment for her. And then she did it up again nervously and quickly. Once she faltered for a minute and stood still while a tear or two splashed on the worn red carpet.

On went her old brown jacket; on went her old brown hat. 11
With a whirl of skirts and with the brilliant sparkle still in her eyes, she fluttered out the door and down the stairs to the street.

Where she stopped the sign read: "Mme. Sofronie. Hair 12
Goods of All Kinds." One flight up Della ran, and collected her-self, panting, before Madame, large, too white, chilly and hardly looking the "Sofronie."

"Will you buy my hair?" asked Della. 13

"I buy hair," said Madame. "Take yer hat off and let's have a 14
sight at the looks of it."

Down rippled the brown cascade. 15

"Twenty dollars," said Madame, lifting the mass with a prac- 16
tised hand.

"Give it to me quick," said Della. 17

Oh, and the next two hours tripped by on rosy wings. Forget 18
the hashed metaphor. She was ransacking the stores for Jim's present.

She found it at last. It surely had been made for Jim and no 19
one else. There was none other like it in any of the stores, and she had turned all of them inside out. It was a platinum fob chain simple and chaste in design, properly proclaiming its value by substance alone and not by meretricious ornamenta-tion—as all good things should do. It was even worthy of The Watch. As soon as she saw it she knew that it must be Jim's. It was like him. Quietness and value—the description applied to both. Twenty-one dollars they took from her for it, and she hur-ried home with the 87 cents. With that chain on his watch Jim might be properly anxious about the time in any company. Grand as the watch was, he sometimes looked at it on the sly on account of the old leather strap that he used in place of a chain.

When Della reached home her intoxication gave way a little 20
to prudence and reason. She got out her curling irons and
lighted the gas and went to work repairing the ravages made by
generosity added to love. Which is always a tremendous task,
dear friends—a mammoth task.

Within forty minutes her head was covered with tiny, close- 21
lying curls that made her look wonderfully like a truant school-
boy. She looked at her reflection in the mirror long, carefully and
critically.

"If Jim doesn't kill me," she said to herself, "before he takes a 22
second look at me, he'll say I look like a Coney Island chorus
girl. But what could I do—oh, what could I do with a dollar and
eighty-seven cents!"

At 7 o'clock the coffee was made and the frying pan was on 23
the back of the stove hot and ready to cook the chops.

Jim was never late. Della doubled the fob chain in her hand 24
and sat on the corner of the table near the door that he always
entered. Then she heard his step on the stair away down on the
first flight, and she turned white for just a moment. She had a
habit of saying little silent prayers about the simplest everyday
things, and now she whispered: "Please, God, make him think I
am still pretty."

The door opened and Jim stepped in and closed it. He 25
looked thin and very serious. Poor fellow, he was only twenty-
two—and to be burdened with a family! He needed a new overcoat and he was without gloves.

Jim stopped inside the door, as immovable as a setter at the 26
scent of quail. His eyes were fixed upon Della, and there was an
expression in them that she could not read, and it terrified her.
It was not anger, nor surprise, nor disapproval, nor horror, nor
any of the sentiments that she had been prepared for. He simply stared at her fixedly with that peculiar expression on his
face.

Della wriggled off the table and went for him. 27

"Jim, darling," she cried, "don't look at me that way. I had 28
my hair cut off and sold it because I couldn't have lived
through Christmas without giving you a present. It'll grow

again—you won't mind, will you? I just had to do it. My hair grows awfully fast. Say 'Merry Christmas!' Jim, and let's be happy. You don't know what a nice—what a beautiful, nice gift I've got for you."

"You've cut off your hair?" asked Jim, laboriously, as if he had not arrived at that patent fact yet even after the hardest mental labor.   29

"Cut it off and sold it," said Della. "Don't you like me just as well, anyhow? I'm me without my hair, ain't I?"   30

Jim looked about the room curiously.   31

"You say your hair is gone?" he said, with an air almost of idiocy.   32

"You needn't look for it," said Della. "It's sold, I tell you— sold and gone too. It's Christmas Eve, boy. Be good to me, for it went for you. Maybe the hairs of my head were numbered," she went on with a sudden serious sweetness, "but nobody could ever count my love for you. Shall I put the chops on, Jim?"   33

Out of his trance Jim seemed to quickly wake. He enfolded his Della. For ten seconds let us regard with discreet scrutiny some inconsequential object in the other direction. Eight dollars a week or a million a year—what is the difference? A mathematician or a wit would give you the wrong answer. The magi brought valuable gifts, but that was not among them. This dark assertion will be illuminated later on.   34

Jim drew a package from his overcoat pocket and threw it upon the table.   35

"Don't make any mistake, Dell," he said, "about me. I don't think there's anything in the way of a haircut or a shave or a shampoo that could make me like my girl any less. But if you'll unwrap that package you may see why you had me going awhile at first."   36

White fingers and nimble tore at the string and paper. And then an ecstatic scream of joy; and then, alas! a quick feminine change to hysterical tears and wails, necessitating the immediate employment of all the comforting powers of the lord of the flat.   37

For there lay The Combs—the set of combs, side and back, that Della had worshipped for long in a Broadway window. Beautiful combs, pure tortoise shell, with jewelled rims—just the shade to wear in the beautiful vanished hair. They were expensive combs, she knew, and her heart had simply craved and yearned over them without the least hope of possession. And now, they were hers, but the tresses that should have adorned the coveted adornments were gone.

But she hugged them to her bosom, and at length she was able to look up with dim eyes and a smile and say: "My hair grows so fast, Jim!"

And then Della leaped up like a little singed cat and cried, "Oh, oh!"

Jim had not yet seen his beautiful present. She held it out to him eagerly upon her open palm. The dull, precious metal seemed to flash with a reflection of her bright and ardent spirit.

"Isn't it a dandy, Jim? I hunted all over town to find it. You'll have to look at the time a hundred times a day now. Give me your watch. I want to see how it looks on it."

Instead of obeying, Jim tumbled down on the couch and put his hands under the back of his head and smiled.

"Dell," said he, "let's put our Christmas presents away and keep 'em a while. They're too nice to use just at present. I sold the watch to get the money to buy your combs. And now suppose you put the chops on."

The magi, as you know, were wise men—wonderfully wise men—who brought gifts to the Babe in the manger. They invented the art of giving Christmas gifts. Being wise, their gifts were no doubt wise ones, possibly bearing the privilege of exchange in case of duplication. And here I have lamely related to you the uneventful chronicle of two foolish children in a flat who most unwisely sacrificed for each other the greatest treasures of their house. But in a last word to the wise of these days let it be said that of all who give gifts these two were of the wisest. Of all who give and receive gifts, such as they are the wisest. Everywhere they are the wisest. They are the magi.

Focusing on the Story

1 Describe Jim and Della's apartment and lifestyle.

2 What time of year is it? What holiday is coming up? What is Della's problem?

3 How would you describe Jim and Della's marriage?

4 What are the couple's most valued possessions? Why do they sacrifice their most prized possessions to buy each other gifts?

 Interpreting and Evaluating

1 Irony is a result that is the opposite of what might be expected. What's ironic about Jim and Della's situation?

2 What do Jim and Della have that is more valuable than the most expensive gift?

3 In the last paragraph, O. Henry writes that Della and Jim are "two foolish children . . . who most unwisely sacrificed for each other the greatest treasures of their house." Are Jim and Della foolish? Explain.

4 O. Henry says of Jim and Della that "of all who give and receive gifts, such as they are the wisest. . . . They are the magi." What does O. Henry mean by this statement? How are Jim and Della the wisest? How are they the magi?

5 Some critics have called "The Gift of the Magi" a fable. If it is indeed a fable, what is the moral of the story?

6 Are the best gifts necessarily the most expensive? What are some "gifts" that are free?

 Ideas for Writing and Further Discussion

1 Although O. Henry doesn't describe Della's character directly, the reader can infer what kind of person she is through her thoughts and actions. Write a paragraph in which you describe Della's character. Support each personality trait with details from the story.

2 What are some gifts you like to give? Are they unusual? To whom do you like to give gifts? Write a paragraph or two and describe gifts

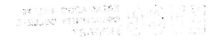

you like to give as well as when and to whom you like to give gifts. How does giving gifts make you feel?

3   Write a few paragraphs about the kinds of gifts you like to receive and when and from whom you like to receive gifts. How do you feel when you receive gifts?

4   Write a paragraph or two describing the best "gift" you ever received. The gift might be something other than an object.

5   People all over the world exchange gifts on various occasions. Why do people give gifts? Is it just tradition? Does it make them feel good, or do they want something in return? Write an essay in which you explore some reasons why people give each other gifts.

Suggested *thesis*: two or three such reasons.

Each *body paragraph* should explore one reason.

6   Perhaps you dislike giving and receiving gifts. Write an essay in which you explore reasons why you dislike giving or receiving (or both) gifts.

Suggested *thesis*: a few such reasons.

Each *body paragraph* should explore one reason only.

Guilt and Innocence

The Confession

Anton Chekhov

About the Author

Anton Chekhov was born in Russia in 1860. He received a medical degree but never practiced medicine. Instead, he devoted his life to writing, and today he stands out as one of the greatest short story writers of all time.

 Something to Think About

How do demands from others affect our judgment? In this story, a thief is caught and confesses his guilt, but is he the only guilty one?

 Words to Keep in Mind

elated *(1)* very happy
miserly *(2)* stingy
haughty *(3)* arrogant
trifling *(7)* of little importance
endure *(10)* tolerate; stand
rubles *(10)* Russian money
guzzle *(13)* drink greedily
gorge *(13)* eat greedily
ethical *(16)* moral

t was a cold clear day. I felt as elated as a cab driver who [1] has been given a gold coin by mistake. I wanted to

---

From *Anton Chekhov: Selected Stories* by Anton Chekhov. © 1960 by Ann Dunnigan. By permission of Dutton Signet, a division of Penguin Putnam, Inc.

laugh, to cry, to pray. I was in seventh heaven: I had just been made a cashier! But I was rejoicing not because I now could get my hands on something—I was not a thief, and would have destroyed anyone who had told me that in time I should be one—I was rejoicing over the promotion and the slight increase in salary, nothing more.

Also I was happy for another reason: on becoming a cashier I 2 suddenly felt as if I were wearing rose-colored glasses. All at once people appeared to have changed. My word of honor! Everyone seemed to have improved! The ugly became beautiful, the wicked, good; the proud became humble, the miserly, generous. It was as if my eyes had been opened, and I beheld all man's wonderful, until now unsuspected qualities. "Strange," I said to myself, either something has happened to them, or I have been stupid not to have noticed these qualities before. How charming everyone is!"

On the day of my promotion, even Z. N. Kazusov changed. 3 He was a member of the board of directors, a haughty, proud man who always ignored the small fry. He approached me and—what had happened to him?—smiling affectionately, he clapped me on the back.

"You're too young to be so proud, my boy. It's unforgiv- 4 able!" he said. "Why don't you ever drop in on us? It's shameful of you not to visit. The young people generally gather at our house, and it's always festive there. My daughters are forever asking me: 'Why don't you invite Gregory Kuzmich, Papa? He's so nice!' But is it possible to get him to come? Well, in any case, I'll try, I told them. I'll ask him. Now, don't give yourself airs, my boy, do come."

Amazing! What had happened to Mr. Kazusov? Had he 5 gone out of his mind? He had always been a regular ogre, and now look at him!

On returning home that same day I was astounded: Mama 6 served not the usual two courses at dinner, but four! For tea in the evening there was jam and white bread. The following day, again four courses, again jam; and when guests dropped in, we drank chocolate. The third day it was the same.

"Mama," I said, "what's the matter with you? Why this 7 burst of generosity? You know, my salary wasn't doubled. The increase was trifling."

Mama looked at me in surprise. "Humph! What do you 8 expect to do with the money—save it?"

God only knows what got into them. Papa ordered a fur 9 coat, bought a new cap, took a relaxing vacation, and began to eat grapes—in winter!

Within a few days I received a letter from my brother. This 10 brother could not endure me. We had parted over a difference of opinion: he considered me a selfish parasite, incapable of self-sacrifice, and for this he despised me. In his letter he now wrote: "Dear brother, I love you, and you cannot imagine what hellish torture our quarrel has caused me. Let us make it up. Let us each extend a hand to the other, and may peace triumph! I beg you! Awaiting your reply, I embrace you and remain your most loving and affectionate brother, Yevlampy." Oh, my dear brother! I answered him saying that I embraced him and rejoiced. Within a week I received a telegram: "Thanks. Happy. Send hundred rubles. Most urgent. Embrace you. Yevlampy." I sent the hundred rubles.

Even she changed. She did not love me. Once when I had 11 made so bold as to hint that I admired her, she laughed in my face. On meeting me a week after my promotion, however, she dimpled, smiled, and looked flustered. "What's happened to you?" she asked, gazing at me. "You've grown so handsome. When did you manage to do that?" And then, "Let's dance. . . ."

Sweetheart! Within a month she had given me a mother-in- 12 law. I had become that handsome! When money was needed for the wedding I took three hundred rubles out of the cash box. Why not take it, when you know you are going to put it back as soon as you receive your raise? At the same time I took out a hundred rubles for Kazusov. He had asked for a loan and it was impossible to refuse him; he was a big wheel in the office and could have anyone fired at a moment's notice.

A week before the arrest it was suggested that I give a party. 13 What the devil, let them guzzle and gorge, if that's what they want! I did not count the guests that evening, but I recall that all eight of my rooms were swarming with people, young and old. There were those before whom even Kazusov had to show humility.

His daughters—the oldest being my treasure—were in dazzling attire. The flowers alone with which they covered themselves cost me over a thousand rubles. It was very festive, with glittering chandeliers, deafening music, and plenty of champagne. There were long speeches and short toasts; one journalist presented me with a poem, another with a song. "We in Russia do not know how to appreciate such men as Gregory Kuzmich," cried Kazusov. "It's a shame! Russia is to be pitied!"   14

All those who were shouting, applauding and kissing me, were whispering behind my back, thumbing their noses at me. I saw their smiles and heard their sighs. "He stole it, the crook!" they whispered, with evil grins. But their sighing and smirking did not prevent them from eating, drinking, and enjoying themselves. Wolves never ate as they did.   15

My wife, flashing gold and diamonds, came up to me and whispered: "They are saying that you stole the money. If it's true, I warn you, I cannot go on living with a thief. I'll leave!" And she smoothed down her five-thousand ruble gown. The devil take them all! That very evening Kazusov had five thousand from me. Yevlampy took an equal amount. "If what they are whispering about you is true," said my ethical brother, as he pocketed the money, "watch out! I will not be brother to a thief!"   16

After the party I drove them all to the country in a sleigh. We finished up at six in the morning. Exhausted, they lay back in the sleigh, and, as they started off for home, cried out in farewell: "Inspection tomorrow! Thanks."   17

My dear ladies and gentlemen, I got caught; or, to state it more fully: yesterday I was respected and honored on all sides. Today I am a scoundrel and a thief. . . . Cry out, now, accuse me, spread the news, judge and wonder. Banish me, write editorials and throw stones, only, please—not everyone, not everyone!   18

Focusing on the Story

1 Who is the narrator (the character who tells the story), and what pronoun is used throughout to identify him?

2 Where is the narrator when he is making his confession?

3 On becoming cashier, Gregory Kuzmich feels "as if [he] were wearing rose-colored glasses" and says that "people appeared to have changed." How have the people changed? What causes the change? Is the change temporary or permanent?

4 Why does Gregory Kuzmich continue to shower people with more and more money? What do they give him in return?

5 What are the people whispering behind Gregory Kuzmich's back? What are they threatening to do if they find out that Gregory Kuzmich is guilty of stealing?

 Interpreting and Evaluating

1 Why does author Anton Chekhov reveal the arrest so early in the story? How would the story be different if told in chronological order or in the order the events happened?

2 Is the narrator the only guilty one? Do his so-called friends know that the money is not his to give away? Explain.

3 The narrator is unable to grasp that his family and "friends" are taking advantage of him. As readers, however, we soon catch on. Why has Chekhov created such a naive narrator? What is the effect of such a naive narrator on the story as a whole?

4 What common human weaknesses does Chekhov expose and mock in this story?

5 Rather than telling his story in an objective way, Gregory Kuzmich uses subjective words and phrases in order to win the reader's understanding and approval. Point out several such biased or slanted words. Do you feel sympathy toward Gregory Kuzmich? Why or why not?

 Ideas for Writing and Further Discussion

1 Most people want to "fit in" and try to do what is expected by the group. Think about your group of friends and peers. Write a narrative composition describing a time when you decided to go along with the group, even though it was against your better judgment. Was the result favorable or disastrous? What did you learn from the experience? (If you don't want to write about yourself, write about someone you know.)

2 Write about a time when you dared stand alone and go against the group because you didn't want to compromise your integrity. Describe what happened. Were you rewarded for your courage? What did you learn from your experience?

It's not necessary to write a formal thesis statement in a narrative essay, but you may wish to start with a general statement that expresses an attitude toward the experience.

3 Peer pressure is not always bad, of course. Write an essay in which you discuss how peer pressure can be both good and bad. To prove your point, use examples from your own life when you or someone you know yielded to peer pressure, or use examples from the story.

Suggested *thesis*: three or four ways peer pressure can be both good and bad.

Each *body paragraph* may develop one such way. (Make one list of how peer pressure can be good and another list of how peer pressure can be bad. Use these lists to organize your body paragraphs.)

Han's Crime

Shiga Naoya

About the Author

Shiga Naoya (Shiga is his last name or family name) was born in Japan in 1883 and is best known for his short stories. In most of his stories, the emphasis is less on what happens and more on how the characters feel. The Japanese refer to his genre as "state-of-mind" fiction. Shiga Naoya died in 1971.

 ### *Something to Think About*

A Chinese juggler and knife-thrower named Han kills his wife during a performance in front of a large audience by driving a knife through her neck. But is this incident an act of premeditated murder and thus perhaps an example of a perfect crime, or is it an accident?

 ### *Words to Keep in Mind*

carotid artery *(1)* main artery that carries blood from the heart to the head

interrogating *(4)* questioning

perplexed *(13)* puzzled

solicitation *(17)* request to do something

disposition *(18)* temperament; personality

detriment *(19)* injury; damage

profligacy *(23)* careless spending; wastefulness

demeanor *(36)* behavior

discord *(44)* disagreement

assertive *(77)* bold; aggressive

grub *(97)* wormlike larva of an insect

alleviate *(105)* make easier to endure; lessen

premonition *(105)* forewarning

conjecture *(117)* guess

plea *(117)* excuse; defense

plausible *(117)* reasonable

I n an unusual incident, a young Chinese juggler called 1
Han severed his wife's carotid artery during a performance with a knife the size of a carver. The young wife died on
the spot. Han was immediately arrested.

The act was witnessed by the owner-manager of the troupe, 2
a Chinese stagehand, the introducer, and an audience of over
three hundred. A policeman, sitting on a chair set up slightly
above and at the edge of the audience, also saw it. But it was not
at all known whether this incident, which had occurred before
so many eyes, was a deliberate act or an accident.

For this performance, Han made his wife stand in front of a 3
thick board the size of a rain shutter. From a distance of twelve
feet, he hurled several of the carver-sized knives, each with a
shout, to form an outline of her body not two inches removed
from it.

The judge commenced by interrogating the owner-manager. 4

"Is that performance a particularly difficult one?" 5

"No. For an experienced performer, it is not that difficult. All 6
that's required is an alert, healthy state of mind."

"If that's so, an incident like this should not have happened 7
even as a mistake."

"Of course, unless one is sure of the performer—extremely 8
sure—one cannot allow the performance."

From *The Paper Door* by Shiga Naoya. (Shiga is the last name.) English transla-
tion used by permission of Lane Dunlop. © 1987 by North Point Press.

"Well, then. Do you think it was a deliberate act?"   9

"No. I don't. The performance requires experience, instinc-   10
tive skill and nothing else. But one cannot say that it will always
come off with a machinelike precision. It's a fact that we never
thought something like this would happen. But I do not think it
is fair, now that it *has* happened, to say that we had considered
the possibility and hold it against us."

"Well, what do you think it was?"   11

"I don't know."   12

The judge was perplexed. There was, here, the fact of homi-   13
cide. But there was absolutely no proof as to whether it was premeditated murder or manslaughter (if the former, the judge
thought, there was never such a cunning murder as this). Next
calling in the Chinese stagehand, who had served with the
troupe longer than Han, the judge questioned him.

"What is Han's ordinary behavior like?"   14

"He's a good person. He doesn't gamble, fool around with   15
other women, or drink. About a year ago, he converted to Christianity. His English is good, and when he has the time he often
reads collections of sermons."

"And his wife?"   16

"She was a good person too. As you know, people of our sort   17
aren't always known for their strict morals. One often hears of
somebody running off with somebody else's wife. Han's wife
was a beautiful woman, although on the small side, and she now
and then got solicitations of that sort. But she never took up with
such people."

"What were their dispositions like?"   18

"Toward others, they were both extremely kind and gentle.   19
They never thought of themselves and never got angry. And
yet" (here the stagehand paused. Thinking a moment, he went
on) "I'm afraid this may be to Han's detriment, but to tell the
truth, strangely enough, those two, who were so kind, gentle,
and self-effacing with others, when it came to their own relationship, were surprisingly cruel to each other."

"Why was that?"   20

"I don't know why."   21

"Had they always been that way?"   22

"No. About two years ago, the wife gave birth. The baby was   23
premature, and died in three days or so. But after that, it was
clear even to us that their relationship was slowly going to the
bad. They would often have arguments over the most trivial
things. At such times, Han would suddenly turn dead pale. But
in the end, no matter what, he always fell silent. He never mis-
treated his wife. Of course, that's most likely because his religion
forbade him to. But sometimes, when you looked at his face,
there was a terrible, uncontrollable anger in it. Once, I suggested
that if things were so bad between them it might be good to get a
divorce. But Han said that even if his wife had reasons for seeking a divorce, he himself had none. Han followed his own will in
the matter. He even said that there was no way he could love his
wife. It was only natural, he said, if a woman he did not love
gradually came not to love him. It was why he took to reading
the Bible and collections of sermons. He seemed to think that by
somehow calming his heart he could correct his fairly unruly
feelings of hatred. After all, he had no reason to hate his wife.
She, too, deserved sympathy. After their marriage, they had
travelled about as road-players for nearly three years. Owing to
an older brother's profligacy, the family back home was already
broken up and gone. Even if she had left Han and gone back,
nobody would have trusted a woman who'd been on the road
four years enough to marry her. Bad as things were, she had no
choice but to stay with Han."

"What is *your* opinion of the incident?"   24

"You mean whether it was deliberate or an accident?"   25

"Yes."   26

"Actually, I've thought a lot about that. But the more I've   27
thought, the more I've come, by degrees, not to understand anything."

"Why is that?"   28

"I don't know why. I really do not. I think anyone would   29
have the same problem. I asked the introducer what he thought,
but he said he didn't know either."

"Well, at the instant it happened, what did you think?"   30

"I thought: He's murdered her. I did think that." 31

"Is that so?" 32

"But the introducer told me that he thought: He's bungled it." 33

"Is that so? But isn't that what he would think, not knowing 34
too much about their relationship?"

"Maybe so. But later, I thought that my thinking he'd mur- 35
dered her might also, in the same way, simply have been
because I knew a good deal about their relationship."

"What was Han's demeanor just then?" 36

"He gave a short cry: 'Aa!' That was what drew my attention 37
to what had happened. The blood suddenly gushed out of the
wife's neck. Even so, she remained upright for a moment. Her
body was held in place by the knife's sticking in the board
behind her. Then, all of a sudden, her knees buckled, the knife
came out and collapsing all together she fell forward. There was
nothing anyone could do. We all of us just went stiff and
watched. But I can't be sure of anything. I didn't have the leisure
to observe Han's demeanor just then. But it seems to me that for
those few seconds he was just like us. It was only afterward that
I thought: He's murdered her at last. Han went dead pale and
stood there with his eyes closed. We drew the curtain down and
tried to revive the woman, but she was already dead. Han, his
face bluish with excitement, blurted out: 'How could I make
such a blunder?' Then he knelt, in a long silent prayer."

"Was his demeanor agitated then?" 38

"It was somewhat agitated." 39

"Good. If I have any further questions, I'll call you." 40

Dismissing the Chinese stagehand, the judge finally had 41
Han himself brought in. Han, his face drawn and pale, was an
intelligent-looking man. It was clear at a glance to the judge that
he was suffering from nervous exhaustion. As soon as Han had
seated himself, the judge said: "I've been questioning the owner-
manager and the stagehand. I will now ask you some questions." Han nodded.

"Have you never loved your wife at all?" 42

"From the day I married her until the day she had the baby, I 43
loved my wife with all my heart."

"Why did the birth become a source of discord?"   44

"Because I knew it wasn't my child."   45

"Do you know who the father was?"   46

"I have an idea it was my wife's cousin."   47

"Did you know the man?"   48

"He was a close friend of mine. It was he who suggested that   49
we get married. He introduced me to her."

"Was there a relationship before she married you?"   50

"Of course there was. The baby was born the eighth month   51
after the marriage."

"The stagehand said it was a premature birth."   52

"That's because I told him it was."   53

"The baby died shortly afterwards?"   54

"Yes."   55

"What was the cause of death?"   56

"It choked at the breast."   57

"Was that a deliberate act of your wife's?"   58

"She said it was an accident."   59

The judge, falling silent, looked intently at Han. Han, eyes   60
lowered in his raised face, waited for the next question.

"Did your wife tell you about the relationship?"   61

"No, she didn't. Nor did I ask her about it. I felt that the   62
baby's death was a judgement on her for what she'd done. I
thought that I myself should be as forgiving as possible."

"But, in the end, you couldn't forgive her?"   63

"That's right. My feeling remained that the baby's death   64
wasn't enough of a judgement. At times, when I thought about it
by myself, I could be rather forgiving. But then, my wife would
come in. She would go about her business. As I looked at her, at
her body, I could not keep down my displeasure."

"You didn't think of divorcing her?"   65

"I often thought I'd like a divorce. But I never said any-   66
thing."

"Why was that?"   67

"I was weak. And my wife had said that if I divorced her she   68
would not survive."

"Did your wife love you?"   69

"She did not love me."   70

"If that was so, why did she say such a thing?"   71

"I think it was from the necessity of going on living. Her   72
brother had broken up the household back home, and she knew
that no respectable man would marry a woman who'd been the
wife of a road-player. And her feet were too small for ordinary
work."

"What were your sexual relations?"   73

"I believe they were probably not much different from those   74
of an average couple."

"Did your wife feel any sympathy for you?"   75

"I can't think she felt any sympathy. I believe that for my   76
wife living with me was an extraordinary hardship. But the
patience with which she endured hardship was beyond what
one would have thought possible even for a man. My wife simply observed, with cruel eyes, the gradual destruction of my life.
My writhing, desperate attempts to save myself, to enter upon
my true life, she coolly, from the side and without the slightest
wish to help, as if surrounding me, looked on at."

"Why were you unable to take a more assertive, resolute   77
attitude?"

"Because I was thinking about various things."   78

"Various things? What sort of things?"   79

"I thought I would act in such a way as to leave no room for   80
error. But, in the end, those thoughts never offered any solution."

"Did you ever think of killing your wife?"   81

Han did not answer. The judge repeated his question. Even   82
then, Han did not answer immediately. Then, he said:

"I'd often thought, before then, that it would be good if she   83
were dead."

"Then, if the law had allowed it, you might have killed her?"   84

"I was afraid of the law, and I had never had such thoughts   85
before. It was merely because I was weak. But even though I was
weak, my desire to live my own life was strong."

"So, after that, you thought about killing your wife?"   86

"I didn't make my mind up to it. But I did think about it."   87

"How long before the incident was this?"   88

"The night before. Toward daybreak."   89

"Had you quarrelled that evening?"   90

"Yes."   91

"What about?"   92

"Something so trivial it isn't worth mentioning."   93

"Tell me anyway."   94

"It was about food. When I'm hungry, I get irritable. The   95
way she dawdled over the preparations for supper made me
angry."

"Did you quarrel more violently than usual?"   96

"No. But I remained excited longer than usual. It was   97
because lately I'd felt intolerably frustrated by the fact that I did
not have a life of my own. I went to bed, but I couldn't sleep at
all. I thought about all sorts of things. I felt as if my present existence in which, like a grub suspended in midair, I looked to one
side and the other, always hesitating, without the courage to
want what I wanted, without the courage to get rid of what was
unbearable, was all due to my relationship with my wife. I could
see no light in my future. A desire to seek the light was burning
inside me. Or, if it was not, it was trying to catch fire. But my
relationship with my wife would not let it. The flame was not
out. It was smouldering, in a fitful, ugly way. What with the pain
and unhappiness of it all, I was being poisoned. When the poisoning was complete, I would die. Although alive, I would be a
dead man. And though this was what I had come to, I was still
trying to put up with it. It would be good if she died—one part
of me kept having that dirty, hateful thought. If this was how
things were, why didn't I kill her? The consequences of such an
act did not trouble me now. I might be put in jail. Who could tell
how much better life in jail might be than this life? I would cross
that bridge when I came to it. It would be enough if, in any way
I could, I broke through whatever came up at the time it came
up. Even if I broke through, and broke through, I might not
break through all the way. But if I went on breaking through
until the day I died, that would be my true life. I almost forgot
that my wife was lying beside me. At last, I grew tired. But even

though I was tired, it was not the sort of fatigue that leads to sleep. My thoughts began to blur. As my tensed up feelings relaxed, my dark thoughts of murder faded away. A feeling of loneliness came over me, as after a nightmare. I even felt pity for my own weak spirit, that the ability to think hard had, in a single night, become so feeble and forlorn. And then, at last, the night was over. It seemed to me that my wife hadn't slept either."

"When you got up, was everything as usual between you?"   98

"Neither of us said a word to each other."   99

"Why didn't you think of leaving your wife?"   100

"Do you mean that as a desired result, it would have come to the same thing?"   101

"Yes."   102

"For me, there was a great difference."   103

Saying this, Han looked at the judge and was silent. The judge, his face softening, nodded.   104

"But, between my thinking about such a thing and actually deciding to kill her, there was still a wide gap. That day, from early morning on, I felt insanely keyed up. Because of my bodily fatigue, my nerves were edgy, without elasticity. Unable to remain still, I stayed outside all morning. I walked about restlessly, away from the others. I kept thinking that no matter what I would have to do something. But I no longer thought of killing her, as I had the night before. And I was not at all worried about that day's performance. If I had been, I would not have chosen that particular act. We had many other acts. Finally, that evening, our turn came. Then also, I was not thinking of such a thing. As usual, I demonstrated to the audience that the knives were sharp by slicing through a piece of paper and sticking a knife into the stage. My wife, heavily made up and wearing a gaudy Chinese costume, came on. Her stage manner was no different than always. Greeting the audience with a winsome smile, she stepped up to the thick board and stood bolt upright with her back to it. A knife in my hand, I stood at a set distance straight across from her. For the first time since the night before, we exchanged looks. Only then did I realize the danger of having chosen this act for tonight. Unless I practiced the utmost   105 care, I thought, there would be trouble. I must alleviate, as best I could, the day's restless agitation and my strained, edgy nerves. But no matter how I tried, a weariness that had eaten into my heart would not let me. I began to feel that I could not trust my own arm. Closing my eyes, I attempted to calm myself. My body started to sway. The moment came. I drove in the first knife above her head. It went in slightly higher than usual. Then I drove in one knife each under the pits of her arms which were raised to shoulder level. As each knife left my fingertips, something clung to it an instant, as if to hold it back. I felt as if I no longer knew where the knives would go in. Each time one hit, I thought: Thank God. Calm down, calm down, I thought. But I could feel in my arm the constraint that comes from a thing's having become conscious. I drove in a knife to the left of her throat. I was about to drive in the next one to the right, when suddenly a strange look came over her face. She must have felt an impulse of violent fear. Did she have a premonition that the knife about to fly at her would go through her neck? I don't know. I only felt that face of violent fear, thrown back at my heart with the same force as the knife. Dizziness struck me. But even so, with all my strength, almost without a target, as though aiming in the dark, I threw the knife . . ."

The judge was silent. 106

"I've killed her at last, I thought." 107

"How do you mean? That you'd done it on purpose?" 108

"Yes. I suddenly felt as if I had." 109

"Afterwards, you knelt by the body in silent prayer . . . ?" 110

"That was a trick that occurred to me at the moment. I knew 111 everyone thought I seriously believed in Christianity. While pretending to pray, I was thinking about what attitude I should take."

"You felt sure that what you'd done was intentional?" 112

"Yes. And I thought right away I could make out it was an 113 accident."

"But why did you think it was deliberate murder?" 114

"Because of my feelings, which were unhinged." 115

"So you thought you'd skillfully deceived the others?" 116

"Thinking about it later, I was shocked at myself. I acted sur-   117
prised in a natural manner, was considerably agitated, and also
displayed grief. But any perceptive person, I believe, could have
seen that I was playacting. Recalling my behavior, I sweated
cold sweat. That night, I decided that I would have to be found
innocent. First of all, I was extremely encouraged by the fact that
there was not a scrap of objective proof of my crime. Everyone
knew we'd been on bad terms, of course, so there was bound to
be a suspicion of murder. I couldn't do anything about that. But
if I insisted, throughout, that it was an accident, that would be
the end of it. That we'd gotten along badly might make people
conjecture, but it was no proof. In the end, I thought, I would be
acquitted for lack of evidence. Thinking back over the incident, I
made up a rough version of my plea, as plausible as possible, so
that it would seem like an accident. Soon, though, for some reason, a doubt rose up in me as to whether I myself believed it was
murder. The night before, I had thought about killing her, but
was that alone a reason for deciding, myself, that it was murder?
Gradually, despite myself, I became unsure. A sudden excitement swept over me. I felt so excited I couldn't sit still. I was so
happy, I was beside myself. I wanted to shout for joy."

"Was it because you yourself could now believe that it was   118
an accident?"

"No. I'm still unsure of that. It was because it was com-   119
pletely unclear, even to myself, which it had been. It was
because I could now tell the truth and be found innocent. Being
found innocent meant everything to me now. For that purpose,
rather than trying to deceive myself and insisting that it was an
accident, it was far better to be able to be honest, even if it meant
saying I didn't know which it was. I could no longer assert that
it was an accident, nor, on the other hand, could I say that it was
a deliberate act. I was so happy because come what may it was
no longer a question of a confession of guilt."

Han fell silent. The judge, also, was silent for a moment.   120
Then, as if to himself, he said: "On the whole, it seems to be the
truth." And then: "By the way, do you not feel the slightest sor-
row about your wife's death?"

"None whatsoever. And up to now, no matter what my feel- 121
ings of hatred for her, I never imagined that I'd be able to talk so
cheerfully about her death."

"That will be all. You may step down," the judge said. Han, 122
after a slight wordless bow, left the room.

The judge felt an excitement, he could not put a name to it, 123
surge up in him.

Quickly, he took up his pen. And, then and there, he wrote: 124
"Innocent."

 Focusing on the Story

1   Describe the relationship between Han and his wife. What caused
their relationship to deteriorate?

2   Soon after their marriage, Han's wife had a baby. How did Han
feel about the baby? Why did he feel the way he did? What happened
to the baby?

3   How does the stagehand describe Han and his wife? How do the
owner-manager and the stagehand think the incident happened?

4   How had Han spent the night before the performance? How did he
spend the morning of the performance? How did he feel immediately
before and after his wife's death?

5   How does Han himself explain the incident? Why does he change
his mind?

 Interpreting and Evaluating

1   The first few paragraphs of the story sound like a newspaper
account. What effect does such an objective tone have on the story?
Instead of focusing on the plot, what does the author want the reader
to focus on?

2   Why does the author make a point of the fact that Han had converted to Christianity and that he read collections of sermons?

3   The story is written by a Japanese writer for a Japanese audience,
yet the main character is Chinese. What might be a reason for making
Han a different nationality?

4   The reader is given clues of both guilt and innocence along the way. If this had been a trial by jury and you had been on that jury, what would your verdict have been? Give reasons for your answer.

5   What do you think Han's life will be like after this incident? Is there such a thing as a perfect crime?

 Ideas for Writing and Further Discussion

1   The title of the story is "Han's Crime." If Han in fact committed a crime, what was his crime? Write a paragraph in which you explore the answer to this question.

2   Write a paragraph in which you defend Han's action. Look for evidence in the story that points to Han's innocence.

3   Take the opposite stand and argue against Han's innocence. Point to evidence in the story that shows that Han is guilty of murder and should be punished.

4   Try to seriously observe an ordinary situation around you. You may for example observe a child playing in a park or on the beach, or you may observe an argument between your neighbors or a dispute between a store clerk and a customer. Try to imagine how the people feel. Write a short story of your own in which you focus on how the people feel.

Horse Thief

Erskine Caldwell

 ## Something to Think About

How can a small mischief, an innocent lie, lead to serious trouble?

 ## Words to Keep in Mind

calico *(1)* spotted
bridle *(3)* head gear for controlling a horse
shy *(13)* jump or move suddenly from being startled
pommel *(13)* post on the front of a Western saddle
halter *(13)* leather or rope headband used for tying a horse
hitched *(14)* tied the horse

I didn't steal Lud Moseley's calico horse.

People all over have been trying to make me out a thief, but anybody who knows me at all will tell you that I've never been

From *Vanity Fair,* November 1933. © 1933 by Conde Nast Publications, Inc.
© renewed 1960 by Erskine Caldwell. Reprinted by permission of McIntosh and Otis, Inc.

in trouble like this before in all my life. Mr. John Turner will tell you all about me. I've worked for him, off and on, for I don't know exactly how many years. I reckon I've worked for him just about all my life, since I was a boy. Mr. John knows I wouldn't steal a horse. That's why I say I didn't steal Lud Moseley's, like he swore I did. I didn't grow up just to turn out to be a horse thief.

Night before last, Mr. John told me to ride his mare, Betsy. I said I wanted to go off a little way after something, and he told me to go ahead and ride Betsy, like I have been doing every Sunday night for going on two years now. Mr. John told me to take the Texas saddle, but I told him I didn't care about riding saddle. I like to ride with a bridle and reins, and nothing else. That's the best way to ride, anyway. And where I was going I didn't want to have a squeaking saddle under me. I wasn't up to no mischief. It was just a little private business of my own that nobody has got a right to call me down about. I nearly always rode saddle Sunday nights, but night before last was Thursday night, and that's why I didn't have a saddle when I went.

Mr. John Turner will tell you I'm not the kind to go off and get into trouble. Ask Mr. John about me. He has known me all my life, and I've never given him or anybody else trouble.

When I took Betsy out of the stable that night after supper, Mr. John came out to the barnyard and asked me over again if I didn't want to take the Texas saddle. That mare, Betsy, is a little rawboned, but I didn't mind that. I told Mr. John I'd just as lief ride bareback. He said it was all right with him if I wanted to get sawn in two, and to go ahead and do like I pleased about it. He was standing right there all the time, rubbing Betsy's mane, and trying to find out where I was going, without coming right out and asking me. But he knew all the time where I was going, because he knows all about me. I reckon he just wanted to have a laugh at me, but he couldn't do that if I didn't let on where I was headed. So he told me it was all right to ride his mare without a saddle if I didn't want to be bothered with one, and I opened the gate and rode off down the road toward Bishop's crossroads.

3

4

5

That was night before last—Thursday night. It was a little 6 after dark then, but I could see Mr. John standing at the barnyard gate, leaning on it a little, and watching me ride off. I'd been plowing that day, over in the new ground, and I was dog-tired. That's one reason why I didn't gallop off like I always did on Sunday nights. I rode away slow, letting Betsy take her own good time, because I wasn't in such a big hurry, after all. I had about two hours' time to kill, and only a little over three miles to go. That's why I went off like that.

Everybody knows I've been going to see Lud Moseley's 7 youngest daughter, Naomi. I was going to see her that night. But I couldn't show up there till about nine thirty. Lud Moseley wouldn't let me come to see her but once a week, on Sunday nights, and night before last was Thursday. I'd been there to see her three or four times before on Thursday nights that Lud Moseley didn't know about. Naomi told me to come to see her on Thursday nights. That's why I had been going there when Lud Moseley said I couldn't come to his house but once a week. Naomi told me to come anyway, and she had been coming out to the swing under the trees in the front yard to meet me.

I haven't got a thing in the world against Lud Moseley. Mr. 8 John Turner will tell you I haven't. I don't especially like him, but that's to be expected, and he knows why. Once a week isn't enough to go to see a girl you like a lot, like I do Naomi. And I reckon she likes me a little, or she wouldn't tell me to come to see her on Thursday nights, when Lud Moseley told me not to come. Lud Moseley thinks if I go to see her more than once a week that maybe we'll take it into our heads to go get married without giving him a chance to catch on. That's why he said I couldn't come to his house but once a week, on Sunday nights.

He's fixing to have me sent to the penitentiary for twenty 9 years for stealing his calico horse, Lightfoot. I reckon he knows good and well I didn't steal the horse, but he figures he's got a chance to put me out of the way till he can get Naomi married to somebody else. That's the way I figure it all out, because every-body in this part of the country who ever heard tell of me knows

I'm not a horse thief. Mr. John Turner will tell you that about me. Mr. John knows me better than that. I've worked for him so long he even tried once to make me out as one of the family, but I wouldn't let him do that.

So, night before last, Thursday night, I rode off from home   10
bareback, on Betsy. I killed a little time down at the creek, about a mile down the road from where we live, and when I looked at my watch again, it was nine o'clock sharp. I got on Betsy and rode off toward Lud Moseley's place. Everything was still and quiet around the house and barn. It was just about Lud's bed-time then. I rode right up to the barnyard gate, like I always did on Thursday nights. I could see a light up in Naomi's room, where she slept with her older sister, Mary Lee. We had always figured on Mary Lee's being out with somebody else, or maybe being ready to go to sleep by nine thirty. When I looked up at their window, I could see Naomi lying across her bed, and Mary Lee was standing beside the bed talking to her about something. That looked bad, because when Mary Lee tried to make Naomi undress and go to bed before she did, it always meant that it would take Naomi another hour or more to get out of the room, because she had to wait for Mary Lee to go to sleep before she could leave. She had to wait for Mary Lee to go to sleep, and then she had to get up and dress in the dark before she could come down to the front yard and meet me in the swing under the trees.

I sat there on Betsy for ten or fifteen minutes, waiting to see   11
how Naomi was going to come out with her sister. I reckon if we had let Mary Lee in on the secret she would have behaved all right about it, but on some account or other Naomi couldn't make up her mind to run the risk of it. There was a mighty chance that she would have misbehaved about it and gone straight and told Lud Moseley, and we didn't want to run that risk.

After a while I saw Naomi get up and start to undress. I   12
knew right away that that meant waiting another hour or longer for her to be able to come and meet me. The moon was starting to rise, and it was getting to be as bright as day out there in the

barnyard. I'd been in the habit of opening the gate and turning Betsy loose in the yard, but I was scared to do it night before last. If Lud Moseley should get up for a drink of water or something, and happen to look out toward the barn and see a horse standing there, he would either think it was one of his and come out and lock it in the stalls, or else he would catch on it was me out there. Anyway, as soon as he saw Betsy, he would have known it wasn't his mare, and there would have been the mischief to pay right there and then. So I opened the barn door and led Betsy inside and put her in the first empty stall I could find in the dark. I was scared to strike a light, because I didn't know but what Lud Moseley would be looking out the window just at that time and see the flare of the match. I put Betsy in the stall, closed the door, and came back outside to wait for Naomi to find a chance to come out and meet me in the swing in the yard.

It was about twelve thirty or one o'clock when I got ready to   13
leave for home. The moon had been clouded, and it was darker than everything in the barn. I couldn't see my hand in front of me, it was that dark. I was scared to strike a light that time, too, and I felt my way in and opened the stall door and stepped inside to lead Betsy out. I couldn't see a thing, and when I found her neck, I thought she must have slipped her bridle like she was always doing when she had to stand too long to suit her. I was afraid to ride her home without a lead of some kind, because I was scared she might shy in the barnyard and start tearing around out there and wake up Lud Moseley. I felt around on the ground for the bridle, but I couldn't find it anywhere. Then I went back to the stall door and felt on it, thinking I might have taken it off myself when I was all excited at the start, and there was a halter hanging up. I slipped it over her head and led her out. It was still so dark I couldn't see a thing, and I had to feel my way outside and through the barnyard gate. When I got to the road, I threw a leg over her, and started for home without wasting any more time around Lud Moseley's place. I thought she trotted a little funny, because she had a swaying swing that made me slide from side to side, and I didn't have a saddle pommel to hold on to. I was all wrought up about getting away from

there without getting caught up with, and I didn't think a thing about it. But I got home all right and slipped the halter off and put her in her stall. It was around one or two o'clock in the morning then.

The next morning after breakfast, when I was getting ready to catch the mules and gear them up to start plowing in the new ground again, Lud Moseley and three or four other men, including the sheriff, came riding lickety-split up the road from town and hitched at the rack. Mr. John came out and slapped the sheriff on the back and told him a funny story. They carried on like that for nearly half an hour, and then the sheriff asked Mr. John where I was. Mr. John told him I was getting ready to go off to the new ground, where we had planted a crop of corn that spring, and then the sheriff said he had a warrant for me. Mr. John asked him what for, a joke or something? And the sheriff told him it was for stealing Lud Moseley's calico horse, Lightfoot. Mr. John laughed at him, because he still thought it just a joke, but the sheriff pulled out the paper and showed it to him. Mr. John still wouldn't believe it, and he told them there was a mix-up somewhere, because, he told them, I wouldn't steal a horse. Mr. John knows I'm not a horse thief. I've never been in any kind of trouble before in all my life.

They brought me to town right away and put me in the cell room at the sheriff's jail. I knew I hadn't stole Lud Moseley's horse, and I wasn't scared a bit about it. But right after they brought me to town, they all rode back and the sheriff looked in the barn and found Lud Moseley's calico horse, Lightfoot, in Betsy's stall. Mr. John said things were all mixed up, because he knew I didn't steal the horse, and he knew I wouldn't do it. But the horse was there, the calico one, Lightfoot, and his halter was hanging on the stall door. After that they went back to Lud Moseley's and measured my foot tracks in the barnyard, and then they found Betsy's bridle. Lud Moseley said I had rode Mr. John's mare over there, turned her loose, and put the bridle on his Lightfoot and rode off. They never did say how come the halter got to Mr. John's stable, then. Lud Moseley's stall door was not locked, and it wasn't broken down. It looks now like I forgot to shut it tight when I put Betsy in, because she got out someway and came home of her own accord sometime that night.

Lud Moseley says he's going to send me away for twenty years, where I won't have a chance to worry him over his youngest daughter, Naomi. He wants her to marry a widowed farmer over beyond Bishop's crossroads who runs twenty plows and who's got a big white house with fifteen rooms in it. Mr. John Turner says he'll hire the best lawyer in town to take up my case, but it don't look like it will do much good, because my footprints are all over Lud Moseley's barnyard, and his Lightfoot was in Mr. John's stable.

I reckon I could worm out of it someway, if I made up my mind to do it. But I don't like to do things like that. It would put Naomi in a bad way, because if I said I was there seeing her, and had put Betsy in the stall to keep her quiet, and took Lightfoot out by mistake in the dark when I got ready to leave—well, it would just look bad, that's all. She would have to say she was in the habit of slipping out of the house to see me after everybody had gone to sleep, on Thursday nights, and it would just look bad all around. She might take it into her head someday that she'd rather marry somebody else than me, and by that time she'd have a bad name for having been mixed up with me—and slipping out of the house to meet me after bedtime.

Naomi knows I'm no horse thief. She knows how it all happened—that I rode Lud Moseley's calico horse, Lightfoot, off by mistake in the dark, and left the stall door unfastened, and Betsy got out and came home of her own accord.

Lud Moseley has been telling people all around the courthouse as how he is going to send me away for twenty years so he can get Naomi married to that widowed farmer who runs twenty plows. Lud Moseley is right proud of it, it looks like to me, because he's got me cornered in a trap, and maybe he will get me sent away sure enough before Naomi gets a chance to tell what she knows is true.

But, somehow, I don't know if she'll say it if she does get the chance. Everybody knows I'm nothing but a hired man at Mr.

John Turner's, and I've been thinking that maybe Naomi might not come right out and tell what she knows, after all.

I'd come right out and explain to the sheriff how the mix-up 21 happened, but I sort of hate to mention Naomi's name in the mess. If it had been a Sunday night, instead of night before last, a Thursday, I could—well, it would just sound too bad, that's all.

If Naomi comes to town and tells what she knows, I won't 22 say a word to stop her, because that'll mean she's willing to say it and marry me.

But if she stays at home, and lets Lud Moseley and that wid- 23 owed farmer send me away for twenty years, I'll just have to go, that's all.

I always told Naomi I'd do anything in the world for her, 24 and I reckon this will be the time when I've got to prove whether I'm a man of my word or not.

 Focusing on the Story

1   Who is the narrator (the character who tells the story), and where is he when he is telling the story? To whom is he talking?

2   Why did the narrator have to be furtive (sneaky) about meeting his girlfriend, Naomi, on Thursday nights? How did they manage to meet?

3   Who is Lud Moseley, and how does he feel about the narrator? Why does he feel this way? How does Mr. John Turner, the farmer the narrator works for, feel about the narrator?

4   Summarize the events that led to Lud Moseley's calico horse, Lightfoot, ending up in Mr. John Turner's stable.

5   How did Betsy get home? How did John Turner respond to Lud Moseley's accusations?

 Interpreting and Evaluating

1   Do you feel sympathy toward the narrator? Is he really a common thief, or is he being railroaded by Lud Moseley? Explain.

2   The narrator uses ungrammatical phrases such as "it don't look like it will do much good." How do such phrases together with his actions reveal his character traits? Why does he repeat himself so much? How does the language in the story identify the setting (time and place) of the story?

3　Should the narrator tell the sheriff the whole story? Is he carrying his loyalty to Naomi too far? What would you do in that situation?

4　Based on your own knowledge of human nature, what's the likelihood of Naomi eventually coming to the narrator's rescue? What does your response say about your attitude toward people?

5　What is the main point of this story? Are there any lessons, underlying messages, or themes here, and if so, what are they?

 Ideas for Writing and Further Discussion

1　What events led to the narrator's predicament? What could he have done to avoid his arrest? Write an essay in which you explore some of the main mistakes the narrator made that led to his miserable condition, and offer suggestions about how he could have avoided making such mistakes and thus saved himself.

Suggested *thesis*: two or three such errors and suggestions about how he could have avoided them and what he could have done instead.

Each *body paragraph* should look at one mistake and give one positive suggestion.

2　Analyze the narrator's character. What character flaws led to his misfortune? Write an essay in which you explore two or three of the narrator's character traits or two or three groups of related traits and show how these qualities or traits led to his predicament.

Suggested *thesis*: two or three such character traits or groups of traits.

Each *body paragraph* should look at one trait or groups of related traits and give examples from the story to illustrate how this character trait led to his trouble.

3　One of Benjamin Franklin's epigrams states that honesty is the best policy. Do you agree or disagree with this saying? Take a stand and write an essay in which you agree or disagree with this statement. Give examples from your own experience to support your point.

Suggested *thesis*: two or three examples that support your point.

Each *body paragraph* should introduce one such example and show how it proves that honesty is the best policy (or how honesty is not always the best policy if the latter is your point).

4   Have you or someone you know ever been in a similar situation to the narrator's? Describe a time when you or someone you know told a seemingly innocent untruth that led to more serious trouble. How old were you? Why did it seem appropriate to be sneaky at the time? How did the situation escalate? What was the outcome? What lesson did you learn?

It's not necessary to write a formal thesis statement in a narrative essay, but you may wish to start with a general statement that introduces the event and expresses your attitude toward the experience.

The Schoolteacher's Guest

Isabel Allende

About the Author

Isabel Allende, born in 1942, is Chilean but left her homeland after the U.S.-backed military coup in 1973, in which her uncle, President Salvador Allende, was killed. She now lives near San Francisco.

 Something to Think About

Is justice served by demanding an eye for an eye, a tooth for a tooth, and, by extension, a life for a life?

 Words to Keep in Mind

weary *(9)* tired
palate *(9)* roof of the mouth
unwavering *(9)* steady
indulge *(9)* to give in to a wish; to be lenient with
vocation *(9)* a call to perform a certain function
viscous *(10)* sticky
pus *(10)* yellowish matter produced by an infection
putrefaction *(10)* rotting
tenacious *(11)* persistent, stubborn
bestowed *(11)* given
arbiter *(17)* person selected to settle a dispute
adobe *(17)* sun-dried clay bricks

mesmerized *(17)* spellbound, hypnotized, fascinated

medlar *(20)* small tree with hard brown fruit

decrepit *(20)* worn out

lurch *(20)* sudden rolling

machete *(22)* large knife with a heavy blade used to cut sugarcane, for example

lethargy *(38)* sluggishness, lack of energy

elation *(38)* extreme joy

furtively *(39)* secretly

malign *(39)* evil, harmful

engendered *(39)* generated

exalted *(44)* filled with pride or joy

complicity *(44)* partnership in wrongdoing

zeal *(44)* intense enthusiasm

T he schoolteacher Inés entered The Pearl of the Orient, 1
deserted at this hour, walked to the counter where Riad
Halabí was rolling up a bolt of bright-flowered cloth, and
announced to him that she had just cut off the head of a guest in
her boardinghouse. The merchant took out his white handkerchief and clapped it to his mouth.

"What did you say, Inés?" 2

"Exactly what you heard, Turk." 3

"Is he dead?" 4

"Of course." 5

"And now what are you going to do?" 6

"That's what I came to ask *you*," she replied, tucking back a 7
stray lock of hair.

"I think I'd better close the store," sighed Riad Halabí. 8

Reprinted with the permission of Scribner, a division of Simon & Schuster,
from *The Stories of Eva Luna* by Isabel Allende. Translated from the Spanish by Margaret Sayers Peden. © 1989 by Isabel Allende. English transla-
tion © 1991 by Macmillan Publishing Company.

The two had known each other so long that neither could 9
remember the exact number of years, although both recalled
every detail of the day their friendship had begun. At the time,
Halabí had been one of those salesmen who wander the byways
offering their wares, a commercial pilgrim without compass or
fixed course, an Arab immigrant with a false Turkish passport,
lonely, weary, with a palate split like a rabbit's and a subsequent
longing to sit in the shadows. She had been a still-young woman
with firm hips and proud shoulders, the town's only schoolteacher, and the mother of a twelve-year-old son born of a fleeting love affair. The boy was the center of the schoolteacher's life;
she cared for him with unwavering devotion but, barely mask-
ing her inclination to indulge him, applied to him the same
norms of discipline she demanded of the other schoolchildren.
She did not want anyone to be able to say she had brought him
up badly; at the same time, she hoped to negate the father's
legacy of waywardness and instead form her son to be of clear
mind and generous heart. The very evening on which Riad
Halabí had driven into Agua Santa from one side of town, from
the other a group of boys had carried in the body of schoolteacher Inés's son on an improvised stretcher. He had walked
onto someone's property to pick up a fallen mango, and the
owner, an outsider whom no one really knew, had fired a blast
from his rifle meaning to scare the boy away but drilling a black
hole in the middle of his forehead through which his life rapidly
escaped. At that moment, the salesman had discovered his vocation for leadership and, without knowing how, had found himself at the center of things, consoling the mother, organizing the
funeral as if he were a member of the family, and calming the
people to prevent them from tearing the perpetrator limb from
limb. Meanwhile, the murderer, realizing that his life would be
worth very little if he remained there, had fled, meaning never to
return.

It was Riad Halabí who the following morning was at the 10
head of the crowd that marched from the cemetery to the place
where the boy had fallen. All the inhabitants of Agua Santa had
spent that day hauling mangoes, which they threw through the

windows until the house was filled from floor to ceiling. After a few weeks, the sun had fermented the fruit, which burst open, spilling a viscous juice and impregnating the walls with a golden blood, a sweetish pus, that transformed the dwelling into a fossil of prehistoric dimensions, an enormous beast in process of putrefaction, tormented by the infinite diligence of the larvae and mosquitoes of decomposition.

The death of the boy, the role Riad Halabí had played during those days, and the welcome he had received in Agua Santa, had determined the course of his life. He forgot his nomadic ancestry and remained in the village. There he opened a business, The Pearl of the Orient. He married, was widowed, married a second time, and continued his trade, while his reputation for being a just man steadily increased. Inés, in turn, educated several generations of children with the tenacious affection she would have bestowed upon her son, until her energies were spent; then she stepped aside for teachers who arrived from the city with new primers, and retired. After leaving the schoolroom, she felt as if she had aged suddenly, as if time were accelerating; the days passed so quickly that she could not remember where the hours had gone. 11

"I go around in a daze, Turk. I'm dying and don't even know it," she commented. 12

"You're as healthy as you ever were, Inés," replied Riad Halabí. "The problem is that you're bored. You should not be idle." And he suggested she add a few rooms to her house and take in guests: "We don't have a hotel in this town." 13

"We don't have tourists, either," she added. 14

"A clean bed and warm breakfast are a blessing for travelers." 15

And so they had been, primarily for the truckdrivers for National Petroleum, who stayed the night in her boardinghouse when the fatigue and tedium of the road had filled their head with hallucinations. 16

The schoolteacher Inés was the most respected matron in all Agua Santa. She had taught the town's children for several decades, which granted her the authority to intervene in all their lives and take them by the ear when she felt it necessary. Girls 17 brought their boyfriends for her approval, husbands and wives came to her with their marital disagreements; she was counselor, arbiter, and judge in all the town's problems. Her authority, in fact, was mightier than that of the priest, the doctor, or the police. No one stopped her from the exercise of that power. On one occasion she had stalked into the jail, passed the Lieutenant without speaking, snatched the keys from a nail on the wall, and removed from a cell one of her students who had been jailed after a drunken spree. The officer had tried to stand in her way, but she had shoved him aside and marched the boy outside by the back of his collar. Once in the street, she had given him a couple of smacks and assured him that the next time this happened she would lower his pants and give him a spanking he would never forget. The day that Inés came to tell Riad Halabí she had killed one of her clients, he did not doubt for a moment that she was serious, because he knew her too well. He took her arm and walked with her the two blocks that separated The Pearl of the Orient from her house. It was one of the grandest buildings in town, adobe and wood, with a wide veranda where hammocks were hung during the hottest siestas, and ceiling fans in every room. At that hour the house seemed to be empty; only one guest sat in the parlor drinking beer, mesmerized by the television.

"Where is he?" whispered the Arab merchant.   18

"In one of the back rooms," Inés replied, not even lowering   19
her voice.

She led him to the row of rooms she rented—all joined by   20
an arcade with purple morning-glories climbing the columns and pots of ferns hanging from the beams—bordering a patio planted with medlar and banana trees. Inés opened the last door and Riad Halabí entered a room in deep shadow. The shutters were closed, and it was a moment before he saw on the bed the corpse of an inoffensive-looking old man, a decrepit stranger swimming in the puddle of his own death, his trousers stained with excrement, his head hanging by a strip of ashen flesh, and wearing a terrible expression of distress, as if apologizing for all the disturbance and blood, and for the uncommon bother of

having allowed himself to be murdered. Riad Halabí sat down on the room's only chair, his eyes on the floor, trying to control the lurch of his stomach. Inés remained standing, arms across her chest, calculating that it would take her two days to wash up the stains and at least two more to rid the room of its odor of feces and fear.

"How did you do it?" Riad Halabí asked finally, wiping the 21 sweat from his forehead.

"With the machete for harvesting coconuts. I came up 22 behind him and lopped off his head with one swing. He never knew what hit him, poor man."

"Why?" 23

"I had to do it. It was fate. This old man had very bad luck. 24 He never meant to stop in Agua Santa; he was driving through town and a rock shattered his windshield. He came to pass a few hours here while the Italian down at the garage found another windshield. He's changed a lot—we've all grown older, I guess—but I recognized him instantly. I've been waiting all these years; I knew he would come sooner or later. He's the man with the mangoes."

"May Allah protect us," murmured Riad Halabí. 25

"Do you think we should call the Lieutenant?" 26

"Not on your life; why do you say that?" 27

"I'm in the right. He killed my boy." 28

"The Lieutenant wouldn't understand that, Inés." 29

"An eye for an eye and a tooth for a tooth, Turk. Isn't that 30 what your religion teaches?"

"But that's not how the law works, Inés." 31

"Well, then, we can fix him up a little and say he committed 32 suicide."

"Don't touch him. How many guests do you have in the 33 house?"

"Just that truckdriver. He'll be on his way as soon as it's cool; 34 he has to drive to the capital."

"Good. Don't take in any more guests. Lock the door to this 35 room and wait for me. I'll be back tonight."

"What are you going to do?" 36

"I'll take care of this in my own way."   37

Riad Halabí was sixty-five years old, but he had conserved   38
his youthful vigor and the same spirit that had positioned him at
the head of the throng the day he arrived in Agua Santa. He left
the schoolteacher's house and walked rapidly to the first of several visits he was to make that afternoon. Soon after, a persistent
murmur began to spread through the town. The inhabitants of
Agua Santa wakened from the lethargy of years, excited by the
unbelievable news that was being repeated from house to house,
an insuppressible buzzing, information that strained to be uttered in shouts, gossip that by the very need to be held to a murmur was conferred special status. Before sunset you could sense
in the air the restless elation that for several years would be a
characteristic of the town, one incomprehensible to strangers
passing through, who could find nothing extraordinary in this
town that had the appearance of being an insignificant back-
water like so many others on the edge of the jungle. Early in the
evening, men began arriving at the tavern; women carried their
kitchen chairs out to the sidewalk and sat down to enjoy the cool
air; young people gathered en masse in the plaza, as if it were
Sunday. The Lieutenant and his men casually made their rounds
and then accepted the invitation of the girls at the whorehouse
who were celebrating a birthday, they said. By nightfall there
were more people in the street than on All Saints' Day; all of
them were so studiously occupied in their activities that they
seemed to be practicing a part in a movie: some were playing
dominoes, others were drinking and smoking on the street corners, some couples were out for a stroll, hand in hand, mothers
were running after their children, grandmothers peering nosily
from open doorways. The priest lighted the lamps in the parish
church and rang the bells signaling a novena to Saint Isidro Martyr, but no one was in the mood for that kind of devotion.

At nine-thirty there was a meeting in the house of school-   39
teacher Inés: the Turk, the town doctor, and four young men she
had taught from the first grade and who were now hefty veter-
ans back from military service. Riad Halabí led them to the back
room, where they found the cadaver covered with insects: the

window had been left open and it was the hour of the mosquitoes. They stuffed the victim in a canvas sack, wrestled it out to
the street, and unceremoniously threw it into the back of Riad
Halabí's truck. They drove through the town, right down the
main street, waving, as usual, to anyone they happened to see.
Some neighbors returned their salutation with more than ordinary enthusiasm, while others pretended not to notice them,
furtively giggling, like children surprised at some mischief.
Beneath brilliant moonlight the men drove to the spot where
many years before the son of the schoolteacher Inés had stooped
down for the last time to pick up a mango. The overgrown property sat amid the malign weeds of neglect, decayed by time and
bad memories, a tangled hill where mangoes had grown wild,
where fruit had dropped from the trees and taken root in the
ground, giving birth to new clumps that had in turn engendered
others, until an impenetrable jungle had been created that had
swallowed up fences, path, even the ruins of the house, of which
only a lingering trace of the odor of marmalade remained. The
men lighted their kerosene lanterns and plunged into the dense
growth, hacking a path with their machetes. When they felt they
had gone far enough, one of them pointed to a spot and there, at
the foot of a gigantic tree weighed down with fruit, they dug a
deep hole in which they deposited the canvas sack. Before shov-
eling back the dirt, Riad Halabí spoke a brief Muslim prayer,
because he knew no other. When they got back to town at mid-
night, they found that no one had gone to bed; lights were blaz-
ing in every window, and people were circulating through the
streets.

Meanwhile, the schoolteacher Inés had scrubbed the walls   40
and furniture in the back room with soap and water; she had
burned the bedclothing, aired the house, and was waiting for
her friends with a fine dinner and a pitcher of rum and pine-
apple juice. The meal was eaten to the accompaniment of merry
chatter about the latest cockfights—a barbaric sport according to
the schoolteacher, but less barbaric, the men alleged, than the
bullfights in which a Colombian matador had just lost his liver.
Riad Halabí was the last to say goodbye. That night, for the first

time in his life, he felt old. At the door, the schoolteacher Inés took his hands and for a moment held them in hers.

"Thank you, Turk," she said. 41

"Why did you come to see me, Inés?" 42

"Because you are the person I love most in this world, and because you should have been the father of my son." 43

The next day the inhabitants of Agua Santa returned to their usual chores exalted by a magnificent complicity, by a secret kept by good neighbors, one they would guard with absolute zeal and pass down for many years as a legend of justice, until the death of the schoolteacher Inés freed us, and now I can tell the story. 44

 Focusing on the Story

1   How and by whom had the only son of schoolteacher Inés been killed? What did the killer do after the murder? What happened to his house?

2   Who was Riad Halabí, and how did he become involved in the affairs surrounding the death of schoolteacher Inés's son the very day he arrived in Agua Santa? Why did Riad Halabí decide to remain in the village?

3   What did schoolteacher Inés do after she retired from teaching?

4   Describe the people who lived in the town of Agua Santa. How did they feel about schoolteacher Inés? How had she helped them over the years?

5   Who was the old traveler that schoolteacher Inés killed? Who did Inés go to for help? Why weren't the police called?

 Interpreting and Evaluating

1   Why do you think the old traveler stopped in Agua Santa? Didn't he recognize the town? Was it fate? Support your opinion.

2   How did many of the townspeople learn about the murder? How did they feel about it? How did they keep it secret? If you had lived in that town, would you have remained silent? Why or why not?

3   Several people helped Inés get rid of the body. What did they do with it? Why did they participate so willingly? Were they common criminals? Explain.

4   What would have happened if Inés or one of the townspeople had called the police? Was there ever a fear that might happen? Why or why not?

5   According to the narrator, the story has been passed down "for many years as a legend of justice." Was justice served in this case? Is justice served by taking the law into your own hands? Would it have been more just to convict and imprison Inés for the murder? Explain.

 Ideas for Writing and Further Discussion

1   Do you believe in a predetermined destiny or fate? Write about some aspects of your life that you believe have been shaped by fate.

Suggested *thesis*: two or three aspects of your life that you believe have been shaped by fate.

Each *body paragraph* should explore one such aspect.

2   Our system of justice may not be perfect, but it's better than many judicial systems around the world. Write an essay in which you discuss two or three aspects of our judicial system that are designed to make sure that justice is served.

Suggested *thesis*: two or three such aspects.

Each *body paragraph* should take a look at one aspect and show how it's designed to make sure that justice is served.

3   Or you may take the opposite stand: Our forefathers may have had the best intentions when they created our judicial system, but it's slowly falling apart, and today other industrialized countries have a more efficient system than we do. Write an essay in which you discuss two or three flaws in our judicial system that prevent justice from being served.

Suggested *thesis*: two or three such flaws.

Each *body paragraph* should look at one such flaw and give several reasons why it prevents justice from being served.

The Secret

Alberto Moravia

About the Author

Alberto Moravia was born in Rome, Italy, in 1907 and died in 1990. His many novels and short stories often explore human psychology. Novels that have been translated into English include *The Conformist, Contempt*, and *Boredom*.

 Something to Think About

Do most people generally get involved in other people's problems today? If you saw someone lying on the sidewalk, would you stop and ask if you could help? Why are most of us afraid to get involved? When are we most likely to get involved?

 Words to Keep in Mind

quarry *(2)* place where building stones are cut

daisy *(2)* common flower with many white narrow petals around a yellow center

mull over *(5)* think about; ponder

berth *(5)* place to sleep on a ship or vehicle

gauging *(6)* measuring; estimating

goring *(7)* piercing, especially with a horn or sword

foundling *(10)* child of unknown parents who has been found abandoned

Tiber *(12)* river in Italy that flows through Rome

wrought up *(22)* worked up

Don't talk to me about secrets! I had one—and it was the   1
kind that weighs on your conscience like a nightmare.

I am a truck driver. One beautiful spring morning, while   2
hauling a load of lava rock from a quarry near Campagnano to
Rome, I ran square into a man who was coming in the opposite
direction on a motor bike. It was right at the 25 Kilometer
marker on the old Cassia road. Through no fault of his, either. I
had kept going on the wrong side of the road long after having
passed a car, and I was speeding; he was on the right, where he
belonged, and going slow. The truck hit him so hard that I barely
had time to see something black fly through the blue air and
then fall and lie still and black against the soft whiteness of a
daisy field. The motor bike lay on the other side of the road, its
wheels in the air, like a dead bug.

Lowering my head, I stepped down hard on the gas. I tore   3
down the road to Rome and dropped my load at the yard.

The next day the papers carried the news: So-and-so, forty-   4
three years old, a jobber by trade, leaving a wife and several children, had been run down at Kilometer 25 of the Cassia road and
instantly killed. Nobody knew who had struck him. The hit-and-
run driver had fled the scene of the accident like a coward.
That's exactly what the paper said: *like a coward*. Except for those
three little words that burned a hole in my brain, it didn't take
more than four lines to report on what was, after all, only the
death of a man.

During the next couple of days, I could think of nothing else.   5
I know that I am only a truck driver, but who can claim that
truck drivers have no conscience? A truck driver has a lot of
time to mull over his own private business, during the long
hours behind the wheel or lying in the truck's sleeping berth.
And when, as in my case, that private business is not all it ought
to be, thinking can get to be really pretty tough.

From *Roman Tales* by Alberto Moravia. Translated from the Italian by Helen
   Cantarella. Reprinted by permission of Curtis Brown Ltd. © 1957 by Casa
   Editrice Valentino, Bompiani & Co.

One thing in particular kept nagging at me. I just couldn't 6 understand why I hadn't stopped, why I hadn't tried to help the poor guy. I lived the scene over and over again. I would be gauging the distances again before passing that car; I would feel my foot pressing down hard on the accelerator. Then the man's body would come flying up in front of my windshield . . . and at this point I would deliberately block out the picture, as you do at the movies, and I would think, "Now, jam on brakes, jump down, run into the field, pick him up, put him in the bed of the truck and rush him to Santo Spirito Hospital. . . ."

But, you poor fool, you're just dreaming again. I had *not* 7 stopped, I had driven straight on, with head lowered like a bull after a goring.

To make a long story short, the more I thought about that 8 split second when I had stepped on the gas instead of jamming on the brakes, the less I could make it out. Cowardice—that was the word for it all right. But why does a man who has, or at least thinks he has guts, turn into a coward without a moment's warning? That stumped me. Yet the cold hard facts were there: the dead man was really dead; that split second when I might have stopped had passed and was now sinking farther and farther away and no one would ever be able to bring it back. I was no longer the Gino who had passed that car but another Gino who had killed a man and then had run away.

I lay awake nights over it. I grew gloomy and silent and after 9 a while everybody shied away from me at the yard and after work: nobody wants to pass the time with a kill-joy. So I carried my secret around as if it were a hot diamond that you can't entrust to anyone or plant anywhere.

Then, after a while, I began thinking about it less and less 10 and I can even say that there came a time when I didn't think about it at all. But the secret was still stowed away deep down inside me and it weighed on my conscience and kept me from enjoying life. I often thought that I would have felt better if I could have told somebody about it. I wasn't exactly looking for approval—I realized there was no pardon for what I had done— but if I could have told this secret of mine I would have thrown off part of its dead weight onto somebody else who would have helped me carry it. But who could I tell it to? To my friends at the yard? They had other things to worry about. To my family? I had none, being a foundling. My girl friend? She would have been the logical person because, as everybody knows, women are good at understanding you and giving you sympathy when you need it, but unfortunately, I had no girl friend.

II

One Sunday in May I went walking outside the Rome city 11 gates with a girl I had met some time before when I had given her and one of her friends a lift in my truck. She had told me her name and address, and I had seen her again a couple of times. We had enjoyed each other's company, and she had made it clear that she liked me and would be willing to go out with me.

Her name was Iris. She was a lady's maid in the house of 12 some wealthy woman who had lots of servants. I had fallen from the start for her serious little oval face and those great big sad gray eyes of hers. In short, here was just the girl for me in the present circumstances. After we had a cup of coffee at the Exposition Grounds, with all those columns around us, she finally agreed in her shy, silent, and gentle way to go and sit with me in a meadow not far from St. Paul's Gate, where you get a good view of the Tiber and of the new apartment houses lined up on the opposite bank. She had spread out a handkerchief on the grass to keep her skirt from getting dirty and she sat quietly, her legs tucked under her, her hands in her lap, gazing across at the big white buildings on the other side of the river.

I noticed that there were lots of daisies in the grass around 13 us; and like a flash I remembered the soft whiteness of those other daisies among which, just a month earlier, I had seen lying still and dead the man I had struck down. I don't know what got into me but suddenly I couldn't hold back the urge to tell her my secret. If I tell her, I thought, I'll get rid of the load on my chest. She wasn't one of those dizzy, empty-headed girls who, after you've told them a secret, make you feel so much worse than you did before, that you could kick yourself hard for having spilled all you know. She was a nice, understanding person who had doubtless had her share of knocks in life—and they must have been pretty rough knocks if the sad little look on her face meant anything. Just to break the ice, I said to her, in an offhand way: "What are you thinking about, Iris?"

She was just raising her hand to choke back a yawn. Perhaps 14 she was tired. She said: "Nothing."

I didn't let that answer get me down but quickly went on. 15 "Iris, you know that I like you a lot, don't you? That's why I feel that I shouldn't hide anything from you. You've got to know everything about me. Iris, I've got a secret."

She kept on looking at the tall buildings on the other side of 16 the river, all the while fingering a little red lump on her chin, a tiny spring pimple.

"What secret?" she asked. 17

With an effort I got it out: "I've killed a man." 18

She didn't move but kept on poking gently at her chin. Then 19 she shivered all over, as though she had finally understood. "You've killed a man? And you tell me about it just like that?"

"And how else do you expect me to tell you?" 20

She said nothing. She seemed to be looking for something on 21 the ground. I went on. "Let's get this thing straight. I didn't mean to kill him."

Suddenly she found what she wanted: picking a long blade 22 of grass, she put it into her mouth and began chewing on it, thoughtfully. Then, hurriedly, but without hiding anything, I told her about the accident, bringing out the part about my cowardice. I got pretty wrought up in spite of myself, but already I was beginning to feel relieved. I concluded:

"Now tell me what you think about all this." 23

She kept munching on her blade of grass and didn't say a 24 word.

I insisted. "I'll bet that now you can't stand the sight of me." 25

I saw her shrug her shoulders, lightly. "And why shouldn't I 26 be able to stand the sight of you?"

"Well, I don't know. After all, it was my fault that poor guy 27
got killed."

"And it bothers you?" 28

"Yes. Terribly." Suddenly, my throat closed tight as if over a 29
hard knot of tears. "I feel as if I can't go on living. No man can go
on if he thinks he's a coward."

"Was it in the papers?" 30

"Yes. They gave it four lines. Just to say he had been killed 31
and that nobody knew who had hit him."

Suddenly she asked, "What time is it?" 32

"Five-fifteen." 33

Another silence. "Listen, Iris, what does a man have to do to 34
find out what's going on in that mind of yours?"

She shifted the blade of grass from one corner of her mouth 35
to the other and said frankly, "Well, if you must know, there's
nothing on my mind. I feel good and I'm not thinking about
anything."

I couldn't believe my ears. I protested. "It can't be! You must 36
have been thinking something about something. I'm sure of it."

I saw her smile, faintly. "Well, as a matter of fact, I was think- 37
ing about something. But if I tell you, you'll never believe it."

Hopefully, I asked, "Was it about me?" 38

"Good heavens, no! It had absolutely nothing to do with 39
you!"

"What was it, then?" 40

She said slowly, "It was just one of those things that only 41
women think about. I was looking at my shoes and seeing that
they have holes in them. I was thinking that there is a big clear-
ance sale on in Via Cola di Rienzo and that I've got to go there
tomorrow and buy myself a pair of new shoes. There . . . are you
satisfied?"

This time I shut up like a clam, my face dark and brooding. 42
She noticed it and exclaimed: "Oh, dear! You're not mad, are
you?"

I couldn't help blurting out: "Sure, I'm mad. Damn mad. 43
Here I tell you the secret of my life, and it makes so little impression on you I wonder why I didn't keep it to myself!"

This bothered her a bit. "No," she said, "I'm glad you told 44
me about it. It really did make an impression on me."

"Well, what kind of an impression?" 45

She thought it over and then said, scrupulously, "Well, I'm 46
sorry that such a thing had to happen to you. It must have been
awful!"

"Is that all you've got to say?" 47

"I also think," she added, fingering the pimple on her chin, 48
"that it's only right it should bother you."

"Why?" 49

"Well, you said so yourself. You ought to have stopped to 50
help him but you didn't."

"Then you think I am a coward?" 51

"A coward? Well, yes . . . and then no. After all, a thing like 52
that could happen to anybody."

"But you just said that I ought to have stopped!" 53

"You should have; but you didn't. . . ." 54

At this point I saw her glance down at something in the 55
daisies. "Oh, look! How pretty!"

It was an insect, a green and gold beetle, resting on the white 56
petals of a daisy. Suddenly I felt as if I were emptied out—almost
as if that secret over which I had agonized so long had vanished
in the spring air, carried away, lightly, like the white butterflies
that were flitting around in pairs in the sunlight.

Yet with one dogged last hope, I asked: "But tell me, Iris, in 57
your opinion, was I right or wrong not to stop?"

"You were right and you were wrong. Of course, you ought 58
to have stopped. After all, you had run into him. But, on the
other hand, what good would it have done if you had? He was
dead by that time anyway and you would probably have got
into a terrible mess. You were both right and wrong."

After these words, a thought flashed through my mind. 59
"This is the end of Iris. I'll never take her out again. I thought she
was a bright, understanding girl. Instead, she is really nothing
but a half-wit. Enough is enough." I jumped to my feet.

"Come on, let's go," I said. "Otherwise, we'll be late for the 60
movies."

Once inside the theater, in the dark, she slipped her hand 61
into mine, forcing her fingers through mine. I didn't budge. The
film was a love story, a real tear-jerker. When the lights went on
at the end I saw that her big gray eyes were filled with tears and
that her cheeks were wet. "I just can't help it," she said, patting
her face dry with a handkerchief. "Pictures like this always
make me want to cry."

Afterwards we went into a bar and ordered coffee. She 62
pressed so close to me that our bodies touched. Just as the
espresso machine let off a loud stream of steam, she said softly,
"You know that I really like you, don't you?" staring at me with
those great big beautiful eyes of hers.

I felt like answering: "Fine. You really like me, but you'll let 63
me carry the whole weight of my secret alone!" Instead, I said
nothing.

Now I understood that from her, as from everybody else, I 64
could ask only for affection, nothing more than that.

I answered with a sigh, "I like you a lot, too." 65

But already she had stopped listening to me. She was peer- 66
ing at herself in the mirror behind the bar, absorbed and concerned as she fingered the little red lump on her chin.

 Focusing on the Story

1 After Gino, the truck driver, hit the biker, the motorcycle flew
through the air and landed in a daisy field. What did the motorbike
resemble?

2 Why didn't Gino stop to help the biker? Did he deny that it was his
fault?

3 What bothers Gino about the newspaper article?

4 How does Gino finally try to "get rid of the load on his chest"?
Why is it so important for him to tell his secret to somebody?

5 How does Iris react when Gino tells her about the accident? Why
do you think she reacts that way?

Interpreting and Evaluating

1   Is Iris's reaction to Gino's secret similar to or different from Gino's reaction after he hit the biker? Explain.

2   When Gino asks Iris if she thinks he is a coward, she is undecided and says that "after all, a thing like that could happen to anybody." Do you agree that something like this could happen to anybody? Explain. What would you do in a similar situation?

3   Although Iris shows little reaction when Gino tells her his secret, she cries at the movie. How do you account for that?

4   When people suffer in other parts of the world, we often seem eager to help. However, when people are killed in our own cities, most of us just sigh, shrug our shoulders, and lock our doors. Why are we less likely to get involved in problems that are close to us?

5   Should we care more about the people around us? What happens to a society in which no one cares about anyone else?

 Ideas for Writing and Further Discussion

1   Write about a time when you should have gotten involved but didn't. Describe what happened and explain why you decided not to get involved. How do you feel about your decision?

2   Write about a time when you did get involved even though people around you chose to do nothing. What happened? Why did you decide to get involved? What was the outcome? Are you glad that you got involved?

It's not necessary to write a formal thesis statement in a narrative essay, but you may wish to start with a general statement that introduces the event and expresses your attitude toward the experience.

Dealing with Adversity

A Letter to God

Gregorio López y Fuentes

About the Author

Gregorio López y Fuentes was a Mexican journalist and author who died in 1966. A son of a farmer and rancher, he was one of Mexico's most acclaimed novelists during the 1930s and received Mexico's National Prize for Literature for his novel *El Indio* in 1935.

 Something to Think About

What are some personal attributes or qualities that help people cope with adversity?

 Words to Keep in Mind

crest *(1)* high point

corral *(1)* enclosure for keeping animals

centavo *(10)* unit of currency in Mexico and other Latin countries (100 centavos = 1 peso)

hailstones *(11)* frozen raindrops

mortified *(12)* made to feel shame or humiliation

plague *(14)* epidemic disease; disaster

locust *(14)* large grasshopper

resow *(25)* plant again

amiable *(27)* friendly

disillusion *(29)* to take away an illusion or dream; to disappoint

prodigy *(29)* an extraordinary person who inspires wonder

contentment *(31)* satisfaction

T he house—the only one in the entire valley—sat on the 1
crest of a low hill. From this height one could see the
river and, next to the corral, the field of ripe corn dotted with the
kidney-bean flowers that always promised a good harvest.

The only thing the earth needed was a rainfall, or at least a 2
shower. Throughout the morning Lencho—who knew his fields
intimately—had done nothing else but scan the sky toward the
northeast.

"Now we're really going to get some water, woman." 3

The woman, who was preparing supper, replied: 4

"Yes, God willing." 5

The oldest boys were working in the field, while the smaller 6
ones were playing near the house, until the woman called to
them all:

"Come for dinner. . . ." 7

It was during the meal that, just as Lencho had predicted, big 8
drops of rain began to fall. In the northeast huge mountains of
clouds could be seen approaching. The air was fresh and sweet.

The man went out to look for something in the corral for no 9
other reason than to allow himself the pleasure of feeling the
rain on his body, and when he returned he exclaimed:

"Those aren't raindrops falling from the sky, they're new 10
coins. The big drops are ten-centavo pieces and the little ones are
fives. . . ."

With a satisfied expression he regarded the field of ripe corn 11
with its kidney-bean flowers, draped in a curtain of rain. But
suddenly a strong wind began to blow and together with the
rain very large hailstones began to fall. These truly did resemble
new silver coins. The boys, exposing themselves to the rain, ran
out to collect the frozen pearls.

"It's really getting bad now," exclaimed the man, mortified. 12
"I hope it passes quickly."

From *Cuentos campesinos de Mexico* (short stories) by Gregorio López y
  Fuentes. Translated by Donald A. Yates. © 1940 by Gregorio López y
  Fuentes. Reprinted with permission of Angel López Oropeza.

It did not pass quickly. For an hour the hail rained on the 13
house, the garden, the hillside, the cornfield, on the whole valley. The field was white, as if covered with salt. Not a leaf
remained on the trees. The corn was totally destroyed. The flowers were gone from the kidney-bean plants. Lencho's soul was
filled with sadness. When the storm had passed, he stood in the
middle of the field and said to his sons:

"A plague of locusts would have left more than this. . . . The 14
hail has left nothing: this year we will have no corn or beans. . . ."

That night was a sorrowful one: 15

"All our work, for nothing!" 16

"There's no one who can help us!" 17

"We'll all go hungry this year. . . ." 18

But in the hearts of all who lived in that solitary house in the 19
middle of the valley, there was a single hope: help from God.

"Don't be so upset, even though this seems like a total loss. 20
Remember, no one dies of hunger!"

"That's what they say: no one dies of hunger. . . ." 21

All through the night, Lencho thought only of his one hope: 22
the help of God, whose eyes, as he had been instructed, see
everything, even what is deep in one's conscience.

Lencho was an ox of a man, working like an animal in the 23
fields, but still he knew how to write. The following Sunday, at
daybreak, after having convinced himself that there is a protect-
ing spirit, he began to write a letter which he himself would
carry to town and place in the mail.

It was nothing less than a letter to God. 24

"God," he wrote, "if you don't help me, my family and I will 25
go hungry this year. I need a hundred pesos in order to resow
the field and to live until the crop comes, because the hail-
storm . . ."

He wrote "To God" on the envelope, put the letter inside 26
and, still troubled, went to town. At the post office he placed a
stamp on the letter and dropped it into the mailbox.

One of the employees, who was a postman and also helped 27
at the post office, went to his boss laughing heartily and showed
him the letter to God. Never in his career as a postman had he

known that address. The postmaster—a fat, amiable fellow—
also broke out laughing, but almost immediately he turned serious and, tapping the letter on his desk, commented:

"What faith! I wish I had the faith of the man who wrote this 28
letter. To believe the way he believes. To hope with the confidence that he knows how to hope with. Starting up a correspon-
dence with God!"

So, in order not to disillusion that prodigy of faith, revealed 29
by a letter that could not be delivered, the postmaster came up
with an idea: answer the letter. But when he opened it, it was
evident that to answer it he needed something more than good-
will, ink and paper. But he stuck to his resolution: he asked for
money from his employee, he himself gave part of his salary,
and several friends of his were obliged to give something "for an
act of charity."

It was impossible for him to gather together the hundred 30
pesos, so he was able to send the farmer only a little more than
half. He put the bills in an envelope addressed to Lencho and
with them a letter containing only a single word as a signature:
GOD.

The following Sunday Lencho came a bit earlier than usual 31
to ask if there was a letter for him. It was the postman himself
who handed the letter to him, while the postmaster, experienc-
ing the contentment of a man who has performed a good deed,
looked on from the doorway of his office.

Lencho showed not the slightest surprise on seeing the 32
bills—such was his confidence—but he became angry when he
counted the money. . . . God could not have made a mistake, nor
could he have denied Lencho what he had requested!

Immediately, Lencho went up to the window to ask for 33
paper and ink. On the public writing table, he started in to write,
with much wrinkling of his brow, caused by the effort he had to
make to express his ideas. When he finished, he went to the window to buy a stamp which he licked and then affixed to the
envelope with a blow of his fist.

The moment that the letter fell into the mailbox the post- 34
master went to open it. It said:

"God: of the money that I asked for, only seventy pesos 35 reached me. Send me the rest, since I need it very much. But don't send it to me through the mail, because the post-office employees are a bunch of crooks. Lencho."

 Focusing on the Story

1   Who is Lencho, and why is he waiting for rain?

2   How does Lencho feel when it starts to rain? Why does he see the "raindrops falling from the sky" as "new coins"?

3   How does Lencho feel when the rain turns to hail? What happens to the crops? Who does Lencho turn to for help?

4   When the postman and the postmaster first see Lencho's letter, they break out laughing. Then the postmaster turns serious. Why? What does the postmaster decide to do?

5   How does the postmaster feel about his good deed? Why is Lencho disappointed when he gets the answer? What does he do about it?

 Interpreting and Evaluating

1   How do you think the postmaster feels when he reads Lencho's second letter? How would you have felt if you had been the post-master?

2   The reader learns that "Lencho was an ox of a man working like an animal in the fields, but still he knew how to write." What does this quote say about Lencho? Point out other details from which you can make inferences about Lencho's character as well as his economic and social status.

3   Irony results when the outcome is opposite of what is expected. Explain how the ending is ironic.

4   Should Lencho have been happy with the seventy pesos? Is he greedy and ungrateful, assuming God will do as he commands, or is he a victim of ignorance who takes God's existence too literally?

5   Many readers find the ending humorous. What accounts for the humor? How did you react to the ending?

Ideas for Writing and Further Discussion

1   Lencho's strength, hard work, and confidence will undoubtedly help him succeed according to his expectations. What qualities do you think are important for success? Write an essay in which you discuss two or three qualities that are necessary for success.

   Suggested *thesis*: the two or three qualities necessary for success.

   Each *body paragraph* should explore one of the qualities and show how and why it is important for success.

2   Imagine that you have a rich uncle and that you are his favorite niece or nephew. Write him a letter and ask for money to buy something that you have wanted for a long time. Explain to your uncle what you want, and give several good reasons for why you want it.

The Necklace

Guy de Maupassant

About the Author

Born into the French nobility in 1850, Guy de Maupassant grew up to be a brilliant novelist and short story writer. With his quick character sketches, dramatic plots, and surprise endings, he is regarded as one of the most skillful short story writers of all time. He died in a private insane asylum in Paris at age forty-three.

 Something to Think About

Do money and material possessions automatically lead to happiness? What makes a person content?

 Words to Keep in Mind

dowry *(1)* property that a woman brings to a man at marriage
caste *(2)* social class restricted by birth
suppleness *(2)* adaptability to different ideas and circumstances
Breton *(3)* a native of Brittany; a region in western France
antechambers *(3)* smaller rooms that lead into larger rooms
inestimable *(3)* of too great a value to be measured; invaluable
frock *(5)* dress
chagrin *(6)* feeling of embarrassment
elated *(7)* filled with joy
stupefied *(18)* overwhelmed with amazement
dismay *(18)* fear
vexation *(20)* irritation
ecstasy *(40)* extreme happiness

homage *(45)* respect; honor

mantle *(57)* sleeveless coat, cape; cover

clasp *(70)* a fastening, such as a hook or buckle, holding two parts together

francs, louis, sous *(26, 80, 85)* French monetary units

usurer *(80)* a money lender who charges illegally high interest

mansard roof *(84)* common roof in Europe with two slopes on each side; the lower slope is almost vertical

S he was one of those pretty, charming young ladies, born, as if through an error of destiny, into a family of clerks. She had no dowry, no hopes, no means of becoming known, appreciated, loved and married by a man either rich or distinguished; and she allowed herself to marry a petty clerk in the office of the Board of Education.

She was simple, not being able to adorn herself, but she was unhappy, as one out of her class; for women belong to no caste, no race, their grace, their beauty and their charm serving them in the place of birth and family. Their inborn finesse, their instinctive elegance, their suppleness of wit, are their only aristocracy, making some daughters of the people the equal of great ladies.

She suffered incessantly, feeling herself born for all delicacies and luxuries. She suffered from the poverty of her apartment, the shabby walls, the worn chairs and the faded stuffs. All these things, which another woman of her station would not have noticed, tortured and angered her. The sight of the little Breton servant, who cleaned this humble home, awoke in her sad regrets and desperate dreams. She thought of quiet antechambers with their oriental hangings lighted by high bronze torches and of the two great footmen in short trousers who sleep in the large armchairs, made sleepy by the heavy air from the heating apparatus.

She thought of large drawing rooms hung in old silks, of graceful pieces of furniture carrying bric-a-brac of inestimable value and of the little perfumed coquettish apartments made for five o'clock chats with most intimate friends, men known and sought after, whose attention all women envied and desired.

When she seated herself for dinner before the round table, 4 where the tablecloth had been used three days, opposite her husband who uncovered the tureen with a delighted air, saying: "Oh! the good potpie! I know nothing better than that," she would think of the elegant dinners, of the shining silver, of the tapestries peopling the walls with ancient personages and rare birds in the midst of fairy forests; she thought of the exquisite food served on marvelous dishes, of the whispered gallantries, listened to with the smile of the Sphinx while eating the rose-colored flesh of the trout or a chicken's wing.

She had neither frocks nor jewels, nothing. And she loved 5 only those things. She felt that she was made for them. She had such a desire to please, to be sought after, to be clever and courted.

She had a rich friend, a schoolmate at the convent, whom she 6 did not like to visit; she suffered so much when she returned. And she wept for whole days from chagrin, from regret, from despair and disappointment.

One evening her husband returned, elated, bearing in his 7 hand a large envelope.

"Here," he said, "here is something for you." 8

She quickly tore open the wrapper and drew out a printed 9 card on which were inscribed these words:

The Minister of Public Instruction and Madame George Rampon- 10 *neau ask the honor of M. and Mme Loisel's company Monday evening, January 18, at the Minister's residence.*

Instead of being delighted, as her husband had hoped, she 11 threw the invitation spitefully upon the table, murmuring:

"What do you suppose I want with that?" 12

"But, my dearie, I thought it would make you happy. You 13 never go out, and this is an occasion, and a fine one! I had a great deal of trouble to get it. Everybody wishes one, and it is very

select; not many are given to employees. You will see the whole
official world there."

She looked at him with an irritated eye and declared impa- 14
tiently:

"What do you suppose I have to wear to such a thing as that?" 15

He had not thought of that; he stammered: 16

"Why, the dress you wear when we go to the theater. It 17
seems very pretty to me."

He was silent, stupefied, in dismay, at the sight of his wife 18
weeping. Two great tears fell slowly from the corners of her eyes
toward the corners of her mouth; he stammered:

"What is the matter? What is the matter?" 19

By a violent effort she had controlled her vexation and re- 20
sponded in a calm voice, wiping her moist cheeks:

"Nothing. Only I have no dress and consequently I cannot 21
go to this affair. Give your invitation to some colleague whose
wife is better fitted out than I."

He was grieved but answered: 22

"Let us see, Matilda. How much would a suitable gown cost, 23
something that would serve for other occasions, something very
simple?"

She reflected for some seconds, making estimates and think- 24
ing of a sum that she could ask for without bringing with it an
immediate refusal and a frightened exclamation from the eco-
nomical clerk.

Finally she said in a hesitating voice: 25

"I cannot tell exactly, but it seems to me that four hundred 26
francs ought to cover it."

He turned a little pale, for he had saved just this sum to buy 27
a gun that he might be able to join some hunting parties the next
summer, on the plains at Nanterre, with some friends who went
to shoot larks up there on Sunday. Nevertheless, he answered:

"Very well. I will give you four hundred francs. But try to 28
have a pretty dress."

The day of the ball approached, and Mme Loisel seemed sad, 29
disturbed, anxious. Nevertheless, her dress was nearly ready.
Her husband said to her one evening:

"What is the matter with you? You have acted strangely for two or three days." 30

And she responded: "I am vexed not to have a jewel, not one stone, nothing to adorn myself with. I shall have such a poverty-laden look. I would prefer not to go to this party." 31

He replied: "You can wear some natural flowers. At this season they look very chic. For ten francs you can have two or three magnificent roses." 32

She was not convinced. "No," she replied, "there is nothing more humiliating than to have a shabby air in the midst of rich women." 33

Then her husband cried out: "How stupid we are! Go and find your friend Madame Forestier and ask her to lend you her jewels. You are well enough acquainted with her to do this." 34

She uttered a cry of joy. "It is true!" she said. "I had not thought of that." 35

The next day she took herself to her friend's house and related her story of distress. Mme Forestier went to her closet with the glass doors, took out a large jewel case, brought it, opened it and said: "Choose, my dear." 36

She saw at first some bracelets, then a collar of pearls, then a Venetian cross of gold and jewels and of admirable workmanship. She tried the jewels before the mirror, hesitated, but could neither decide to take them nor leave them. Then she asked: 37

"Have you nothing more?" 38

"Why, yes. Look for yourself. I do not know what will please you." 39

Suddenly she discovered in a black satin box a superb necklace of diamonds, and her heart beat fast with an immoderate desire. Her hands trembled as she took them up. She placed them about her throat, against her dress, and remained in ecstasy before them. Then she asked in a hesitating voice full of anxiety: 40

"Could you lend me this? Only this?" 41

"Why, yes, certainly." 42

She fell upon the neck of her friend, embraced her with passion, then went away with her treasure. 43

The day of the ball arrived. Mme Loisel was a great success. She was the prettiest of all, elegant, gracious, smiling and full 44

of joy. All the men noticed her, asked her name and wanted
to be presented. All the members of the Cabinet wished to waltz
with her. The minister of education paid her some attention.

She danced with enthusiasm, with passion, intoxicated with   45
pleasure, thinking of nothing, in the triumph of her beauty, in
the glory of her success, in a kind of cloud of happiness that
came of all this homage and all this admiration, of all these
awakened desires and this victory so complete and sweet to the
heart of woman.

She went home toward four o'clock in the morning. Her hus-   46
band had been half asleep in one of the little salons since mid-
night with three other gentlemen whose wives were enjoying
themselves very much.

He threw around her shoulders the wraps they had carried   47
for the coming home, modest garments of everyday wear,
whose poverty clashed with the elegance of the ball costume.
She felt this and wished to hurry away in order not to be
noticed by the other women who were wrapping themselves in
rich furs.

Loisel detained her. "Wait," said he. "You will catch cold out   48
there. I am going to call a cab."

But she would not listen and descended the steps rapidly.   49
When they were in the street they found no carriage, and they
began to seek for one, hailing the coachmen whom they saw at a
distance.

They walked along toward the Seine, hopeless and shiver-   50
ing. Finally they found on the dock one of those old nocturnal
coupés that one sees in Paris after nightfall, as if they were
ashamed of their misery by day.

It took them as far as their door in Martyr Street, and they   51
went wearily up to their apartment. It was all over for her. And
on his part he remembered that he would have to be at the office
by ten o'clock.

She removed the wraps from her shoulders before the mirror   52
for a final view of herself in her glory. Suddenly she uttered a
cry. Her necklace was not around her neck.

Her husband, already half undressed, asked: "What is the   53
matter?"

She turned toward him excitedly: 54

"I have—I have—I no longer have Madame Forestier's   55
necklace."

He arose in dismay: "What! How is that? It is not possible."   56

And they looked in the folds of the dress, in the folds of the   57
mantle, in the pockets, everywhere. They could not find it.

He asked: "You are sure you still had it when we left the   58
house?"

"Yes, I felt it in the vestibule as we came out."   59

"But if you had lost it in the street we should have heard it   60
fall. It must be in the cab."

"Yes. It is probable. Did you take the number?"   61

"No. And you, did you notice what it was?"   62

"No."   63

They looked at each other, utterly cast down. Finally Loisel   64
dressed himself again.

"I am going," said he, "over the track where we went on   65
foot, to see if I can find it."

And he went. She remained in her evening gown, not having   66
the force to go to bed, stretched upon a chair, without ambition
or thoughts.

Toward seven o'clock her husband returned. He had found   67
nothing.

He went to the police and to the cab offices and put an   68
advertisement in the newspapers, offering a reward; he did
everything that afforded them a suspicion of hope.

She waited all day in a state of bewilderment before this   69
frightful disaster. Loisel returned at evening, with his face har-
rowed and pale, and had discovered nothing.

"It will be necessary," said he, "to write to your friend that   70
you have broken the clasp of the necklace and that you will have
it repaired. That will give us time to turn around."

She wrote as he dictated.   71

At the end of a week they had lost all hope. And Loisel, older   72
by five years, declared:

"We must take measures to replace this jewel."   73

The next day they took the box which had inclosed it to the   74
jeweler whose name was on the inside. He consulted his books.

"It is not I, madame," said he, "who sold this necklace; I only   75
furnished the casket."

Then they went from jeweler to jeweler, seeking a necklace   76
like the other one, consulting their memories, and ill, both of
them, with chagrin and anxiety.

In a shop of the Palais-Royal they found a chaplet of dia-   77
monds which seemed to them exactly like the one they had lost.
It was valued at forty thousand francs. They could get it for
thirty-six thousand.

They begged the jeweler not to sell it for three days. And   78
they made an arrangement by which they might return it for
thirty-four thousand francs if they found the other one before
the end of February.

Loisel possessed eighteen thousand francs which his father   79
had left him. He borrowed the rest.

He borrowed it, asking for a thousand francs of one, five   80
hundred of another, five louis of this one and three louis of that
one. He gave notes, made ruinous promises, took money of
usurers and the whole race of lenders. He compromised his
whole existence, in fact, risked his signature without even knowing whether he could make it good or not, and, harassed by anxiety for the future, by the black misery which surrounded him
and by the prospect of all physical privations and moral torture,
he went to get the new necklace, depositing on the merchant's
counter thirty-six thousand francs.

When Mme Loisel took back the jewels to Mme Forestier the   81
latter said to her in a frigid tone:

"You should have returned them to me sooner, for I might   82
have needed them."

She did not open the jewel box as her friend feared she   83
would. If she should perceive the substitution what would she
think? What should she say? Would she take her for a robber?

Mme Loisel now knew the horrible life of necessity. She did   84
her part, however, completely, heroically. It was necessary to pay
this frightful debt. She would pay it. They sent away the maid;
they changed their lodgings; they rented some rooms under a
mansard roof.

She learned the heavy cares of a household, the odious work of a kitchen. She washed the dishes, using her rosy nails upon the greasy pots and the bottoms of the stewpans. She washed the soiled linen, the chemises and dishcloths, which she hung on the line to dry; she took down the refuse to the street each morning and brought up the water, stopping at each landing to breathe. And, clothed like a woman of the people, she went to the grocer's, the butcher's and the fruiterer's with her basket on her arm, shopping, haggling to the last sou her miserable money.   85

Every month it was necessary to renew some notes, thus obtaining time, and to pay others.   86

The husband worked evenings, putting the books of some merchants in order, and nights he often did copying at five sous a page.   87

And this life lasted for ten years.   88

At the end of ten years they had restored all, all, with interest of the usurer, and accumulated interest, besides.   89

Mme Loisel seemed old now. She had become a strong, hard woman, the crude woman of the poor household. Her hair badly dressed, her skirts awry, her hands red, she spoke in a loud tone and washed the floors in large pails of water. But sometimes, when her husband was at the office, she would seat herself before the window and think of that evening party of former times, of that ball where she was so beautiful and so flattered.   90

How would it have been if she had not lost that necklace? Who knows? Who knows? How singular is life and how full of changes! How small a thing will ruin or save one!   91

One Sunday, as she was taking a walk in the Champs Elysées to rid herself of the cares of the week, she suddenly perceived a woman walking with a child. It was Mme Forestier, still young, still pretty, still attractive. Mme Loisel was affected. Should she speak to her? Yes, certainly. And now that she had paid, she would tell her all. Why not?   92

She approached her. "Good morning, Jeanne."   93

Her friend did not recognize her and was astonished to be so familiarly addressed by this common personage. She stammered: 94

"But, madame—I do not know—You must be mistaken."   95

"No, I am Matilda Loisel." 96

Her friend uttered a cry of astonishment: "Oh! my poor 97
Matilda! How you have changed."

"Yes, I have had some hard days since I saw you, and some 98
miserable ones—and all because of you."

"Because of me? How is that?" 99

"You recall the diamond necklace that you loaned me to 100
wear to the minister's ball?"

"Yes, very well." 101

"Well, I lost it." 102

"How is that, since you returned it to me?" 103

"I returned another to you exactly like it. And it has taken us 104
ten years to pay for it. You can understand that it was not easy
for us who have nothing. But it is finished, and I am decently
content."

Mme Forestier stopped short. She said: 105

"You say that you bought a diamond necklace to replace 106
mine?"

"Yes. You did not perceive it then? They were just alike." 107

And she smiled with a proud and simple joy. Mme Forestier 108
was touched and took both her hands as she replied:

"Oh, my poor Matilda! Mine were false. They were not 109
worth over five hundred francs!"

 Focusing on the Story

1 What is the setting (time and place) of the story? How would you
describe the Loisels' lifestyle before the loss of the necklace? How does
it change after the loss?

2 What kind of person is Matilda Loisel before she loses her friend's
necklace? How does she feel about herself? Is she attractive? Why isn't
she happy? Is she spoiled? How does she change during the ten years
after the loss of the necklace?

3 How would you characterize the relationship between Mr. and
Mrs. Loisel before and after the loss of the necklace? How does Mr.
Loisel treat his wife? How does she respond?

Interpreting and Evaluating

1   After the loss of the necklace, appearance and social status seem less important to Matilda. Why?

2   How has the hard work affected Matilda's character? How has her attitude changed at the end of the story? How has her relationship with her husband changed?

3   What, if anything, has Matilda learned from her experience? Does she feel better about herself? Is she more content? Explain.

4   Should Matilda have told her rich friend about the loss of the necklace right away? How might Matilda's life have been different if she had? What would you have done in a similar situation?

5   Maupassant writes, "How singular is life and how full of changes! How small a thing will ruin or save one!" What does the author mean by these statements? Has Matilda been ruined or saved?

6   The ancient Greek physician Hippocrates once said that idleness leads to evil. What does this mean? Do you agree? Explain.

7   Some have accused Guy Maupassant of being a misogynist, or someone who hates women. What, if anything, in the story might support this allegation or accusation?

 Ideas for Writing and Further Discussion

1   Write an essay in which you discuss how Matilda Loisel's life changes after she loses her friend's necklace. Compare her life before the loss with her life after the loss, and point out how the changes help her focus on the more important things in life.

   Suggested *thesis*: several ways that Matilda Loisel changes.

   Each *body paragraph* should explore one way.

2   What makes you happy? Write a paragraph or two about some things that put a smile on your face.

3   Has a seemingly small event ever changed the course of your life? Have you, for example, like the main character in Maupassant's story, lost something important to you? Perhaps you've even had an accident, or perhaps you met someone by chance. Write about a chance event that changed something in your life. Describe what happened, and explain how the event changed your life. Did it change your life for the better or worse?

Myths and Tales

Perseus and the Gorgon's Head

Retold by
Catharine F. Sellew Hinchman

About the Author

Catharine F. Sellew Hinchman is an American writer. Other collections of hers include *Adventures with the Giants* and *Adventures with the Heroes.*

 Something to Think About

Myths are ancient tales whose authors are unknown. Full of drama and adventure, they usually reinforce social values and teach lessons about everyday life. They often try to explain supernatural and natural events and involve gods or godlike characters.

 Fairy tales, folktales, tall tales, legends, and fables may also teach lessons in living but involve people rather than gods. Enjoy the following stories and think about the themes or messages they are trying to convey.

 Words to Keep in Mind

Gorgon *(title)* any of three horrible sisters who had snakes for hair. According to the myth, anyone who looked upon them would turn to stone.

Hercules *(1)* Greek hero famous for his strength

Oracle *(1)* priest or priestess through whom gods gave answers to questions. The answers often had hidden meanings and were difficult to understand.

T here once was a young hero called Perseus. Like the great Hercules, Perseus was the son of a god and an earthly woman. When he was born, the Oracle sent a message to the baby's grandfather, who was king of the land. It warned him that his grandson, Perseus, would be the cause of his death. For the gods knew that when Perseus grew up, he would accidentally kill his grandfather in a dart-throwing contest.

But the grandfather had no way of telling when or how this grandson would cause his death. He was frightened. What could he do? He walked back and forth on the marble floor of his room. How could he get rid of Perseus?

One dark and stormy night, when the wind shrieked and howled so that no other sounds could be heard, the grandfather and two of his strongest servants went into the little boy's room. They grabbed Perseus and his mother, the beautiful Danaë. The men then threw them, struggling and screaming, into a great chest. They tied a heavy rope around it, and the king locked it with a big black iron key. Then he commanded the servants to throw it into the angry sea. Surely now Perseus would die!

The waves washed the chest far out on the sea. First a wave would toss it way up out of the water, and then drop it deep down under another wave. Still another wave would pick it up and whirl it around and around. Perseus and Danaë were thrown from one side of the chest to the other.

Perseus held tightly to his mother, and tried hard not to show how frightened he was. Brave Danaë held him in her arms and told him stories. She pretended they were in a boat, traveling around the world. She told him of the strange and beautiful lands they would visit. And often it made Perseus forget they were locked in a wooden chest.

Then one day a great wave came along and picked up the 6 chest and dashed it with a crash on to the rocky shore of a far-off land. At first Perseus and his mother were frightened because they did not know what had happened. But when they no longer rocked and tipped or were thrown about, they realized that they were on dry land. How could they get out of the chest? They pushed and pushed, and pounded on the lid with their fists, but it would not open.

It happened that a fisherman was walking along the shore 7 and came upon the chest. As he drew near he heard the pounding and muffled cries of Perseus and Danaë.

"What is this?" he said to himself in surprise. 8

Hearing the fisherman's voice, the two in the chest called 9 louder, "Help! Help! Let us out!"

The fisherman pulled out a big knife, cut the rope, and broke 10 open the lid. Out crawled the tired mother and her child. The two clung to each other shivering with the cold. The fisherman felt sorry for them and brought them to his small cottage not far from the shore.

There, for many years Perseus and Danaë stayed with the 11 fisher folk. Perseus soon learned to be a good fisherman, and he and his mother lived happily together. But one day King Polydectes, proud ruler of this far-off land, happened to pass through the little fishing village.

Danaë was in front of the cottage picking a bunch of flowers 12 when the king rode past. Polydectes thought she was very beautiful standing there, with the sunshine falling on her bright hair and her arms full of gay flowers. He stopped to talk to her and fell in love with her.

Polydectes did not know that Danaë had a son, and when he 13 met Perseus, he was angry. Perseus did not like Polydectes either, and he knew that his mother did not love the proud king or want to marry him. But what could she do? No one dared say no to anything the king asked.

Since King Polydectes did not like Danaë's son he decided to   14
get rid of him. He told Perseus he must bring him the head of a
monster called Medusa. Now, Polydectes knew that only a god
or goddess could do this and that no human being would be
able to. He did not know that Perseus was the son of a god.

Perseus set out on this dangerous adventure. He knew   15
he had to do something to keep his mother from marrying a
man she hated. If he could return with Medusa's head, and surprise the wicked king, he was sure he would be able to save
Danaë.

Medusa, he knew, was the name of one of the three monsters   16
called Gorgons who lived in a cave somewhere near the sea.
Once, Medusa had been a beautiful girl with long golden hair.
She had been so proud of her hair that she had even dared to say
that it was more beautiful than the shining locks of the wise goddess Minerva. This had made Minerva angry and she had punished the maiden by turning her into an ugly monster. Her
golden ringlets had become hissing serpents!

Medusa was so terrible to look upon that no living thing   17
could behold her without turning instantly into stone. All along
the sides of her dark and gloomy cave stood stony men and animals who had looked at her face. Who was alive to tell where
that cavern was? How could Perseus find it?

Perseus went to the great Oracle of the gods in Greece and   18
asked its help. But even the Oracle could not tell him where he
could find Medusa's home. It told him to go to the three witch
sisters called the Graeae. They, too, lived in a cave, and they
might be able to help him. So Perseus traveled for many miles
till he came to the place where the Graeae lived.

As he entered he saw the three old sisters crouched together.   19
They wore dark blue cloaks, and their faces were wrinkled with
age. But the strangest thing about them was that they had only
one eye among them. They sat in the middle of the cave rocking
back and forth, and singing a strange sad song. First one old sister would slip the eye into her head and look around, then she
would hand it to the next sister. And so they would pass the
time, hour after hour, day after day.

Perseus crept up behind them. And as one old woman held   20
out the eye to her sister, Perseus snatched it out of her hand! The
three blind women were terrified when they found the eye was
gone. They shrieked and screamed, and called upon the gods to
help them.

"Who has stolen our eye? Give us back our eye!" they kept   21
crying. "It is our only eye! We cannot see." And they clutched at
the air with their bony fingers and blamed each other for keeping the eye. At last they heard a strange voice.

"I took your eye," Perseus said, "and I will not give it back to   22
you until you tell me where I can find the terrible Medusa, and
how I can cut off her head."

"Who are you?" The three old women cried out as they   23
turned in the direction of his voice.

"I am Perseus," the voice said. "How can I kill Medusa? You   24
must tell me, or you will never see again!" The three sisters put
their heads together and began to whisper. Perseus watched
them hopefully. But he could not hear what they were saying.

"Do not gaze upon her face or you will be turned to stone,"   25
they screamed at last.

"You must wear the magic helmet of Pluto, the god of the   26
Underworld," said one sister. "When it is upon your head, you
will be invisible."

"You must borrow the winged shoes of Mercury," said the   27
second sister.

"You must ask Minerva to lend you her shield," said the   28
third sister. And then they told him where he could find the terrible Medusa's cave. Perseus thanked them and gave back their
eye. Then he went to pray to the gods for help.

The gods liked this brave young hero, Perseus, and they   29
pitied him because he had to do such a dangerous deed. They
were glad to lend him the things he needed.

Minerva gave him her bright silver shield.   30

"Use this shield of mine for a mirror. Always look in it," she   31
told him. "Then you will never need to look at Medusa's face!"

The young messenger of the gods, Mercury, slipped off his   32
winged shoes.

"Wear these," he said, "and you can fly swiftly above the 33
head of the monster!"

And Pluto, himself, took off his magic helmet and placed it 34
on the head of Perseus.

"Now Medusa will not be able to see you, but do not forget 35
that she still can turn you to stone if you look at her," warned the
god of the dark Underworld.

Then Perseus, with these three wonderful gifts of the gods, 36
set out to find the cave of the Gorgons. He could spring up into
the air, and fly swiftly through the clouds with the winged shoes
on his feet. Perseus flew over sea and land. And, although the
cave was at the very farthermost end of the earth, he reached it
in only a few minutes!

He held the shield at arm's length, and looked up at it to see 37
what he was coming to. The shield was a good mirror. In it he
saw the cave. It was dark and covered with slime. Water trickled
through the cracks in the wall and dripped over the people who
had been turned to stone. Two of the Gorgons sat in gloomy
silence, curled in one of the darkest corners of the cave. But the
third Gorgon walked around and around the cave. She moaned
and cried aloud with grief and horror because she had lost her
beauty. This was Medusa! Her hair that had once been like a
shower of gold was a mass of twisting, squirming snakes.

Perseus was careful never to turn his head. He was afraid 38
that if he did he might look at Medusa. At last the monster grew
tired, and lay down to rest.

This was the chance Perseus was waiting for. He knew that 39
because of the magic helmet he could not be seen, and he
walked boldly but quietly into the cave. He went up close to
Medusa, still careful to use Minerva's shield as a mirror. Then,
quick as a flash, he pulled out his sword and cut off Medusa's
terrible head!

Perseus had carried out the most dangerous part of the com- 40
mands given him by King Polydectes. But he still had to bring
the head to the king without once looking at it. Even now it
could turn him to stone. So he held it high up above his head
and started on his way back to his mother and the wicked king.

The next day the dawn goddess, Aurora, gently parted the black curtains of night. She looked out and saw young Perseus flying back in the early sunlight over land and sea to rescue his mother. He was holding the horrible head of Medusa high in the air.

Just what made Perseus look down, he did not know. It seemed to him that he heard a strange sound. Was it a woman crying? Or was it just the gentle morning breeze? What he saw was a beautiful maiden chained to a cliff beside the sea.

She was dressed in a long white gown, and her dark hair fell softly over her shoulders. Tears slipped down her pale face as the cold waves washed over her bare feet. What a sad sight it was! Perseus started to fly down to her.

Then he remembered that this fair maiden must never see Medusa's head or she, like all the others, would be turned to stone. Quickly he dropped down on one of the cliffs out of her sight. He took off his cloak, and, always careful not to look at what he was doing, wrapped the snaky head in it and hung it on his belt. Now, no one could gaze upon the Gorgon's face. Now, he might be able to help the girl tied to the cliff. Perseus flew over to her.

"Why are you chained to this rock?" he asked.

The maiden was at first too shy to speak. Finally she said, "There is a horrible dragon that comes to our land. The Oracle says that if I am given to this dragon it will not come back any more to frighten our people." And with that she burst into tears. As soon as she finished speaking the water began to leap and splash round the rock.

Out of the green sea sprang a terrible dragon! He was covered with shiny black scales. His eyes were red and fire burst from his nostrils. His sharp white teeth shone in the sunlight. The maiden screamed and covered her face with trembling hands.

Perseus flew into the air from the rock where he was standing. With the help of the wings on his heels he hovered over the roaring dragon. He thrust his sharp sword between the scales around the dragon's neck. With a loud cry the monster sprang into the air, blood spurting from the wound. Again Perseus plunged the sword between the black scales. And again! And again! The water was red with blood. The air rang with the fearful cries of the dragon. Finally, Perseus struck the monster over the head with all his strength. The beast writhed and twisted, and with a gasp sank into the ocean.

"You have saved my life!" cried the beautiful young girl. She 49
told him that her name was Andromeda. "How can I thank you?" she asked.

Perseus kissed her and begged her to marry him. That was 50
all the thanks he asked. So they joyfully went back to Andromeda's palace. Her mother and father were very happy and grateful to have their daughter safe again. A great feast was prepared to celebrate the wedding and there was much singing and dancing.

However, before Andromeda had been chained to the rock 51
a man named Phineus had wanted to marry her. He had given her up when he learned that she was to be sacrificed to the terrible dragon. He was not very brave, and he was afraid to try to save her. But when he heard that Perseus had killed the dragon and that Andromeda was safe, he still wanted her for his wife.

He gathered together all the men in his court and they 52
rushed to Andromeda's palace and into the wedding feast. Phineus tried to carry Andromeda away with him. But Perseus and the servants in the palace bravely fought them off. The banquet hall was in an uproar. The women screamed and the men shouted. The clash of swords and shields rang through the palace. Phineus had many more men on his side than Perseus. It looked as though he would win, and would take Andromeda away. Then Perseus thought of Medusa's head that was still in the cloak fastened to his belt.

Springing into the air, he floated over the crowd. He 53
unwrapped the head and held it up.

"Turn away your faces, my friends!" he shouted. And those 54
who were faithful to Perseus turned aside their faces wondering

what he could mean. But Phineus and his followers looked up angrily. Phineus was about to throw a spear at Perseus when his eyes fell on Medusa's face. That very second, while his arm was lifted, he was turned into stone. Another man started to call out. With his mouth still open, the words not yet spoken, he became another stone statue in the banquet hall. And so the enemies of Perseus still stand in the old palace, frozen forever just as they were when they looked at Medusa's head.

Perseus wanted to get back to his own land, and to his mother. This time he made up his mind nothing should stop him on his way. He quickly said good-by to Andromeda's grateful family and friends, and with his young bride started home.   55

It would be hard to describe Danaë's joy at seeing her son again and meeting the beautiful Andromeda. She put her arms around Perseus, and tears of joy ran down her cheeks. She told him how much King Polydectes wanted to marry her. She did not think she would dare say no to him any longer.   56

"I will take care of that, Mother dear," laughed Perseus. He left Danaë with Andromeda, and went to the throneroom of Polydectes. He walked boldly in, and stood before the king.   57

Polydectes jumped up when he saw who it was.   58

"You!" the king cried. "What are you doing here?"   59

"I have come back from my trip to Medusa's cave."   60

"But where is the head?" asked the king, not believing that Perseus had ever really been there.   61

"Right here!" replied Perseus, and he held the head before the king's eyes. Like all the others, the wicked king was turned to stone.   62

Perseus then returned his magic helmet and shield and winged shoes to Pluto, Minerva and Mercury. All the gods seemed very pleased that he had done so well. The wise goddess Minerva took the head of Medusa and placed it in her shield so it could no longer do anyone any harm. Perseus was glad to be rid of the terrible head at last, and he and Andromeda lived happily ever after.   63

Focusing on the Story

1 At the beginning of the story, why did the "king of the land" want to get rid of his grandson, Perseus?

2 The king threw Perseus and his mother Danaë into a great chest. What did he command his servants to do with the chest?

3 In the chest, the frightened Danaë told her son that they were in a boat and that they would visit many strange and beautiful countries. Why did she lie to her son?

4 Where did Danaë and Perseus end up? Who found them?

5 Polydectes, the king of the new land, fell in love with Danaë. How did Polydectes feel about Perseus, and how did Perseus feel about his mother's suitor?

6 What did Polydectes ask Perseus to do?

7 Describe Medusa. Why had the goddess Minerva turned her into an ugly monster? What special power did Medusa have?

8 The great Oracle told Perseus to visit three witch sisters called the Graeae. What was peculiar about the sisters?

9 What items did the sisters recommend that Perseus borrow from Pluto, Mercury, and Minerva? How did he obtain these items, and what did they do for him?

10 How did Perseus avoid looking at Medusa? What did he do to her?

11 On his way back, Perseus saw a beautiful girl, Andromeda, chained to a cliff. Why was she tied to this rock? What did Perseus do to save her?

12 When Perseus brought Andromeda home to her parents, he learned that Andromeda had an old fiancé, Phineus. How did Perseus defeat Phineus and his accomplices?

 Interpreting and Evaluating

1 Like most good stories, this myth includes many different conflicts. What are some of these conflicts?

2 At the end of the story, Perseus killed Polydectes. Should he have spared him? Why or why not? Explain.

3 What can you infer from this myth about the values in Ancient Greek society? What actions did the gods seem to favor? What actions were punished? Do we have some of the same values today?

4 The women in this myth seem to be either exceedingly good and beautiful or very bad and ugly. What can you infer about the Ancient Greeks' attitude toward women from this myth?

5 Myths were told to make sense out of a chaotic world, to teach lessons in living, or simply to entertain. What is the purpose of this myth? Is there more than one purpose?

6 In this myth bravery is rewarded. Is bravery always rewarded? Explain.

 Ideas for Writing and Further Discussion

1 Perseus is described as a young hero because he possessed qualities that the Ancient Greeks admired. Write about a hero in your own life. Why is this person a hero in your opinion? In other words, what important qualities does your hero possess that makes him or her a hero to you? Write an essay in which you discuss reasons why the person you selected is a hero.

Suggested *thesis:* several reasons why he or she is a hero (or several qualities your hero possesses that make him or her your hero).

Each *body paragraph* should explore one reason (or quality or group of qualities).

2 The myth about Perseus is full of excitement and adventure. Write an adventure story of your own. Introduce your characters, describe the setting, and then create a plot that includes lots of action. Write your story in chronological order.

Frigga's Necklace

Retold by
Catharine F. Sellew Hinchman

About the Author

Catharine F. Sellew Hinchman is an American writer. Her books include *Adventures with the Gods* and *Adventures with the Heroes*.

 Something to Think About

A seemingly small event can sometimes lead to disaster. How does the goddess Frigga in this story cause storms, cold weather, ice, and snow to enter the world?

 Words to Keep in Mind

Odin *(1)* head of all the Norse gods, also called All-father
Frigga *(1)* Odin's wife and mother of the gods
Asgard *(3)* home of the Norse gods

Frigga, the queen of the gods, sat beside Odin on the high throne on the top of the world. She was very beautiful, with white plumes in her hair that waved softly in the breeze.

She wore snowy white robes and a golden girdle from which hung a ring of keys. She smiled down at the men and women of the earth and watched over their homes and children.

Often she feasted with the other gods and goddesses, but 2 best of all she loved to spin golden thread and weave clouds of glowing colors to put in the sky. Her spinning wheel was set with jewels that sparkled at night. The people of the earth saw them shining in the sky and called them stars.

Frigga was kind and beautiful, but she was also very vain. 3 She loved new gowns and bright jewelry. She could not be happy unless she was the most beautifully dressed goddess in Asgard.

One day she took out her box of jewels and looked at one 4 necklace after another. None of them were quite brilliant enough or quite the right length. None of them really suited her new gown. She wanted a new necklace.

It should be a necklace of pure gold, she decided. It should 5 be made in such a design that everyone—especially her husband, Odin—would wonder at it. So Frigga sent a messenger down to the workshop of the dwarfs. Those ugly little blacksmiths could make magic things out of the metals and jewels that they dug from the heart of the mountains.

Frigga's messenger went to the most skillful of the dwarfs, 6 and told him what the queen of the gods wanted.

"It must be more beautiful than anything you have ever 7 made," the messenger commanded.

"And all of gold?" asked the dwarf.   8

"Yes, pure gold. You must not use any other metal."   9

"But we do not have enough gold for such a necklace," said 10 the dwarf, shaking his head sadly.

"Then dig deeper into the heart of the mountains until you 11 have found enough. This is an order from Frigga! It is the goddess queen who demands it!"

"I know! I know! But we have already made many orna- 12 ments of gold for that beautiful lady and the other gods and goddesses. We have only a little gold left. Please explain this to her highness. Tell her I will make a necklace of wondrous beauty. It will be made of all the metals of the earth in a design worthy only of the lovely Frigga!"

When the messenger went back and told Frigga what the most skillful dwarf had said she was very disappointed. A necklace of many metals would no doubt be beautiful. But for her new gown—gold, pure gold, was needed. If the dwarfs could not get enough gold, *she* would find some on earth and send it to that most skillful dwarf. 13

Then the beautiful goddess put on her traveling robes and swept down the rainbow bridge. She walked for miles and miles over the earth in search of gold for her necklace. There was a gold ring here. There was a gold bracelet there. But they belonged to the men and women of the earth, whom Frigga loved as though they were her own children. She did not wish to take such things from them. Besides it would take many, many rings and bracelets to make enough gold. 14

At last she came to a statue that stood in a little village. It was much taller than any man of the earth. It shone so brightly that beams of light came from it and threw a dazzling glow for miles around. It was made of pure gold. 15

Frigga cried out with pleasure! Here at last was more than enough gold for her necklace. Just a small piece of the statue would be plenty. As the queen of the gods came closer, she saw it was a statue of her husband, Odin. It looked so much like Odin that for a minute she expected it to speak. She would not have been surprised if it had asked her what she was doing so far from her throne in Asgard. 16

But, no, it was only a dumb statue. She would just break off a piece of gold big enough for the necklace and no one would miss it. If it were missed, no one would know where it had gone. The dwarf would have already made it into a beautiful necklace for her. 17

The men and women of the earth had made this statue of the All-father so that they might worship him. Odin had been very pleased. He had been kind to those faithful men and women, and had protected them from the evil of the frost giants. In the dark of the night he often walked through the village and smiled 18 upon the simple homes full of sleeping men and women. Even in the dark the gold statue glowed and threw a warm light upon the stones of the street.

It was on such a night that Odin discovered a piece of gold 19 had been taken from his statue. He was very angry!

"What is this?" he shouted. "Who has dared to steal gold 20 from my statue? He shall pay heavily for this. Do not think I am unable to discover the thief!"

Odin's voice rang through the silent village. Dark clouds 21 rolled across the night sky. A fierce wind howled and tugged at the roofs of the little houses. And the men, women and children pulled their blankets over their heads and trembled with fear.

"The thief shall pay for this!" Odin roared again. The wind 22 picked up his words and howled, "Thief! Thief!" And the giants in the dark cold depths of the earth laughed and shook their fists with joy. Evil was again in the world and the great Odin was angry.

Now the most skillful dwarf had already turned the stolen 23 piece of gold into a necklace for Frigga. Never had there been such a handsome necklace. It had been hammered and twisted and carved in a way that immediately caught everyone's attention. All the goddesses gazed upon it with envy and wonder. Even Odin praised it.

"It is a thing of rare beauty," he had said. "Fit only for my 24 queen to wear." And he had smiled upon Frigga and she was very happy.

But now Odin did not smile. He did not seem to notice 25 Frigga or what she wore. He spoke seldom and sat upon his throne scowling down upon the earth. Nothing Frigga said or did could rouse him. She began to be afraid. What would happen if he ever found out she had stolen the gold?

Finally Odin went back to the statue. He wrote magic verses 26 upon it so that the next morning it would be able to speak and name the thief.

When Frigga saw him writing upon the statue from her 27 throne in Asgard, her face went white with terror. What could she do? Odin might never forgive her. Should she confess? No.

His anger would be too terrible to bear. He must never know the truth. But how could she stop him from finding out?

Quickly, while Odin was still down on the earth, Frigga fled 28 to the land of the dwarfs. Down the dark, winding underground passages she stumbled. Loose stones slipped under her feet and several times she almost fell. Down and down she went until she came to the workshop of the blackest dwarf. The most skillful dwarf could not help her this time. The blackest dwarf must do the daring deed.

"Help me! Help me!" she begged as the tears ran down her 29 pale cheeks. The little dwarf gazed at her in surprise. His face was grimy and red from working. His little green eyes gleamed with cunning. But his heart softened as he looked at the frightened goddess.

"What can I do?" he croaked. "I have no power against the 30 great Odin."

"You must think of something," sobbed Frigga. "The statue 31 will speak my name in the morning. Break the statue! You must break the statue!"

"I wouldn't dare," said the dwarf. 32

"Please! Please!" begged the goddess. And the great queen 33 smiled through her tears upon the little black dwarf. "You are the only living creature who can help me. Is your heart hard and cold like the frost giants'? Will you leave me to face my husband's fearful rage, when by using your great cunning you can save me? Tell me you are not so cruel! Please destroy the statue!" Again Frigga wept.

"Well," said the blackest dwarf slowly, "perhaps I can help 34 you. I would not do such a thing for anyone else. I shall be taking a great chance."

"Surely you are not afraid to take a chance," Frigga said. She 35 smiled at him and the rosy color came back into her cheeks. "I shall never forget your great kindness." Then she ran back up the dark passages and on up to her throne in Asgard.

The next morning Odin returned to the statue. Alas! It was 36 broken into a million gold pieces scattered upon the ground. There was no longer any statue to speak the name of the thief.

Odin stood looking down at the heap of gold with his one blue eye. As Frigga watched him from her throne, her heart stood still with fear. But Odin only stood there silently thinking. She could not see the black rage that darkened his brow, for his head was bent.

What was he thinking? Had he guessed now who the thief 37
was? But how could he? What was he doing—standing there?

And then the great king of the gods turned on his heel. He 38
did not look back. Without looking to the right or to the left he walked straight ahead until he disappeared from sight.

Days passed. Weeks passed. Months passed. Odin did not 39
return. Frigga sat alone on her high throne. The frost giants laughed with glee. Now who would rule the world and protect the people from evil? They blew cold blasts upon the earth. Storms raged on land and sea. The sun no longer warmed the world. Ice and snow covered everything.

In Asgard all was confusion and sadness. Odin had left the 40
world. His silent anger was worse than any rage Frigga or the other gods and goddesses had ever known.

Frigga remembered the happy days before she had risked so 41
much for the sake of vanity. The necklace no longer seemed beautiful. Because of it she had brought on all this evil and trouble. She knew that Odin had left the world because evil had been done, even though he might not have learned the name of the thief. She wept and prayed all night and all day for his forgiveness.

Then one day, when they had given up hope of ever seeing 42
Odin again, the great All-father returned. He smiled upon Frigga and the other gods and goddesses. He looked down upon the dark, cold world. And, as he gazed, the ice began to melt. The sun began to break through the gray clouds. The plants began to grow. Odin was no longer angry. All was forgiven. The frost giants grumbled and growled, but there was nothing they could do.

Frigga never knew whether Odin had guessed the whole 43
truth, but she never wore the beautiful gold necklace again.

Focusing on the Story

1   Describe Frigga. What did she look like, and what was she like as a person?

2   One day Frigga decided she wanted a new necklace for her new gown. Why did she feel she had to have such a special necklace?

3   Frigga sent a messenger to a skillful blacksmith to make the necklace, but there was a problem. What was the problem?

4   On her journey across the earth, Frigga finally came to a large statue that stood in a village. What did Frigga take from the statue? How did her husband Odin feel when he discovered the theft?

5   Why did Frigga ask one of the dwarfs to destroy the statue?

6   Who represents goodness in the story? Who represents evil?

 Interpreting and Evaluating

1   Frigga has both positive and negative qualities. List some positive qualities, as well as several negative ones.

2   Because of the necklace, Frigga faces both external and internal conflicts. What are they and how does she resolve them?

3   How does Frigga persuade the dwarf to destroy the statue? Why does the dwarf agree to do it?

4   Name some common persuasion techniques used today. How are they similar or different to the way Frigga appeals to the dwarf to break the statue?

5   A small thing can lead to a heap of trouble. How does Frigga's seemingly innocent desire cause evil to enter the world?

 Ideas for Writing and Further Discussion

1   Why did Frigga feel compelled to hide the truth from Odin? Write a paragraph in which you discuss two or three reasons why Frigga decided not to tell Odin about the theft.

2   Has a small event in your life ever caused you big trouble? You may, for example, have told a seemingly harmless lie and before you knew it, you were in a big mess. Think about a time when a seemingly small event developed into a big problem and write a paragraph or two about it. Start by describing the event and show how it escalated into a big problem.

Three Strong Women

Retold by Clauss Stamm

About the Author

Claus Stamm has lived in Japan, where he heard this story and decided to retell it in English. He has also written *The Very Special Badgers: A Tale of Magic from Japan.*

 Something to Think About

Wrestling has long been a popular sport in Japan. Is strength measured only by physical force?

 Words to Keep in Mind

furrow *(20)* deep, narrow groove in the ground as made by a plow

chortle *(57)* laugh softly with a deep voice; chuckle

rheumatism *(52)* condition characterized by inflammation or pain in muscle, joints, or fibrous tissue

waggle *(87)* move back and forth; wag

L ong ago, in Japan, there lived a famous wrestler, and he was on his way to the capital city to wrestle before the Emperor. 1

From *Three Strong Women,* © 1962 by Claus Stamm, renewed © 1990 by Claus Stamm and Kazue Mizumura. Published by Viking Penguin, a division of Penguin Putnam, Inc.

He strode down the road on legs thick as the trunks of 2
small trees. He had been walking for seven hours and could,
and probably would, walk for seven more without getting
tired.

The time was autumn, the sky was a cold, watery blue, the 3
air chilly. In the small bright sun, the trees along the roadside
glowed red and orange.

The wrestler hummed to himself, "Zun-zun-zun," in time 4
with the long swing of his legs. Wind blew through his thin
brown robe, and he wore no sword at his side. He felt proud that
he needed no sword, even in the darkest and loneliest places.
The icy air on his body only reminded him that few tailors
would have been able to make expensive warm clothes for a
man so broad and tall. He felt much as a wrestler should—
strong, healthy, and rather conceited.

A soft roar of fast-moving water beyond the trees told him 5
that he was passing above a river bank. He "zun-zunned"
louder; he loved the sound of his voice and wanted it to sound
clearly above the rushing water.

He thought: They call me Forever-Mountain because I am 6
such a good strong wrestler—big, too. I'm a fine, brave man and
far too modest ever to say so. . . .

Just then he saw a girl who must have come up from the 7
river, for she steadied a bucket on her head.

Her hands on the bucket were small, and there was a dimple 8
on each thumb, just below the knuckle. She was a round little
girl with red cheeks and a nose like a friendly button. Her eyes
looked as though she were thinking of ten thousand funny stories at once. She clambered up onto the road and walked ahead
of the wrestler, jolly and bounceful.

"If I don't tickle that fat girl, I shall regret it all my life," said 9
the wrestler under his breath. "She's sure to go 'squeak' and I
shall laugh and laugh. If she drops her bucket, that will be even
funnier—and I can always run and fill it again and even carry it
home for her."

He tiptoed up and poked her lightly in the ribs with one 10
huge finger.

"Kochokochokocho!" he said, a fine, ticklish sound in Japa- 11
nese.

The girl gave a satisfying squeal, giggled, and brought one 12
arm down so that the wrestler's hand was caught between it and
her body.

"Ho-ho-ho! You've caught me! I can't move at all!" said the 13
wrestler, laughing.

"I know," said the jolly girl. 14

He felt that it was very good-tempered of her to take a joke 15
so well, and started to pull his hand free.

Somehow, he could not. 16

He tried again, using a little more strength. 17

"Now, now—let me go, little girl," he said. "I am a very 18
powerful man. If I pull too hard I might hurt you."

"Pull," said the girl. "I admire powerful men." 19

She began to walk, and though the wrestler tugged and 20
pulled until his feet dug great furrows in the ground, he had to
follow. She couldn't have paid him less attention if he had been a
puppy—a small one.

Ten minutes later, still tugging while trudging helplessly 21
after her, he was glad that the road was lonely and no one was
there to see.

"Please let me go," he pleaded. "I am the famous wrestler 22
Forever-Mountain. I must go and show my strength before the
Emperor"—he burst out weeping from shame and confusion—
"and you're hurting my hand!"

The girl steadied the bucket on her head with her free hand 23
and dimpled sympathetically over her shoulder. "You poor,
sweet little Forever-Mountain," she said. "Are you tired? Shall I
carry you? I can leave the water here and come back for it later."

"I do not want you to carry me. I want you to let me go, and 24
then I want to forget I ever saw you. What do you want with
me?" moaned the pitiful wrestler.

"I only want to help you," said the girl, now pulling him 25
steadily up and up a narrow mountain path. "Oh, I am sure
you'll have no more trouble than anyone else when you come up
against the other wrestlers. You'll win, or else you'll lose, and

you won't be too badly hurt either way. But aren't you afraid you might meet a really *strong* man someday?"

Forever-Mountain turned white. He stumbled. He was 26 imagining being laughed at throughout Japan as "Hardly-Ever-Mountain."

She glanced back. 27

"You see? Tired already," she said. "I'll walk more slowly. 28 Why don't you come along to my mother's house and let us make a strong man of you? The wrestling in the capital isn't due to begin for three months. I know, because Grandmother thought she'd go. You'd be spending all that time in bad company and wasting what little power you have."

"All right. Three months. I'll come along," said the wrestler. 29 He felt he had nothing more to lose. Also, he feared that the girl might become angry if he refused, and place him in the top of a tree until he changed his mind.

"Fine," she said happily. "We are almost there." 30

She freed his hand. It had become red and a little swollen. 31 "But if you break your promise and run off, I shall have to chase you and carry you back."

Soon they arrived in a small valley. A simple farmhouse with 32 a thatched roof stood in the middle.

"Grandmother is at home, but she is an old lady and she's 33 probably sleeping." The girl shaded her eyes with one hand. "But Mother should be bringing our cow back from the field— oh, there's Mother now!"

She waved. The woman coming around the corner of the 34 house put down the cow she was carrying and waved back.

She smiled and came across the grass, walking with a lively 35 bounce like her daughter's. Well, maybe her bounce was a little more solid, thought the wrestler.

"Excuse me," she said, brushing some cow hair from her 36 dress and dimpling, also like her daughter. "These mountain paths are full of stones. They hurt the cow's feet. And who is the nice young man you've brought, Maru-me?"

The girl explained. "And we have only three months!" she 37 finished anxiously.

"Well, it's not long enough to do much, but it's not so short a   38
time that we can't do something," said her mother, looking
thoughtful. "But he does look terribly feeble. He'll need a lot of
good things to eat. Maybe when he gets stronger he can help
Grandmother with some of the easy work about the house."

"That will be fine!" said the girl, and she called her grand-   39
mother—loudly, for the old lady was a little deaf.

"I'm coming!" came a creaky voice from inside the house,   40
and a little old woman leaning on a stick and looking very
sleepy tottered out of the door. As she came toward them she
stumbled over the roots of a great oak tree.

"Heh! My eyes aren't what they used to be. That's the fourth   41
time this month I've stumbled over that tree," she complained
and, wrapping her skinny arms about its trunk, pulled it out of
the ground.

"Oh, Grandmother! You should have let me pull it up for   42
you," said Maru-me.

"Hm. I hope I didn't hurt my poor old back," muttered the   43
old lady. She called out, "Daughter! Throw that tree away like a
good girl, so no one will fall over it. But make sure it doesn't hit
anybody."

"You can help Mother with the tree," Maru-me said to   44
Forever-Mountain. "On second thought, you'd better not help.
Just watch."

Her mother went to the tree, picked it up in her two hands,   45
and threw it—clumsily and with a little gasp, the way a woman
throws. Up went the tree, sailing end over end, growing smaller
and smaller as it flew. It landed with a faint crash far up the
mountainside.

"Ah, how clumsy," she said. "I meant to throw it *over* the   46
mountain. It's probably blocking the path now, and I'll have to
get up early tomorrow to move it."

The wrestler was not listening. He had very quietly fainted.   47

"Oh! We must put him to bed," said Maru-me.   48

"Poor, feeble young man," said her mother.   49

"I hope we can do something for him. Here, let me carry   50
him, he's light," said the grandmother. She slung him over her

shoulder and carried him into the house, creaking along with her cane.

The next day they began the work of making Forever-Moun- 51
tain over into what they thought a strong man should be. They gave him the simplest food to eat, and the toughest. Day by day they prepared his rice with less and less water, until no ordinary man could have chewed or digested it.

Every day he was made to do the work of five men, and 52
every evening he wrestled with Grandmother. Maru-me and her mother agreed that Grandmother, being old and feeble, was the least likely to injure him accidentally. They hoped the exercise might be good for the old lady's rheumatism.

He grew stronger and stronger but was hardly aware of it. 53
Grandmother could still throw him easily into the air—and catch him again—without ever changing her sweet old smile.

He quite forgot that outside this valley he was one of the 54
greatest wrestlers in Japan and was called Forever-Mountain. His legs had been like logs; now they were like pillars. His big hands were hard as stones, and when he cracked his knuckles the sound was like trees splitting on a cold night.

Sometimes he did an exercise that wrestlers do in Japan— 55
raising one foot high above the ground and bringing it down with a crash. Then people in nearby villages looked up at the winter sky and told one another that it was very late in the year for thunder.

Soon he could pull up a tree as well as the grandmother. He 56
could even throw one—but only a small distance. One evening, near the end of his third month, he wrestled with Grandmother and held her down for half a minute.

"Heh-heh!" She chortled and got up, smiling with every 57
wrinkle. "I would never have believed it!"

Maru-me squealed with joy and threw her arms around 58
him—gently, for she was afraid of cracking his ribs.

"Very good, very good! What a strong man," said her 59
mother, who had just come home from the fields, carrying, as usual, the cow. She put the cow down and patted the wrestler on the back.

They agreed that he was now ready to show some *real* 60 strength before the Emperor.

"Take the cow along with you tomorrow when you go," 61 said the mother. "Sell her and buy yourself a belt—a silken belt. Buy the fattest and heaviest one you can find. Wear it when you appear before the Emperor, as a souvenir from us."

"I wouldn't think of taking your only cow. You've already 62 done too much for me. And you'll need her to plow the fields, won't you?"

They burst out laughing. Maru-me squealed, her mother 63 roared. The grandmother cackled so hard and long that she choked and had to be pounded on the back.

"Oh, dear," said the mother, still laughing. "You didn't think 64 we used our cow for anything like *work!* Why, Grandmother here is stronger than five cows!"

"The cow is our pet." Maru-me giggled. "She has lovely 65 brown eyes."

"But it really gets tiresome having to carry her back and 66 forth each day so that she has enough grass to eat," said her mother.

"Then you must let me give you all the prize money that I 67 win," said Forever-Mountain.

"Oh, no! We wouldn't think of it!" said Maru-me. "Because 68 we all like you too much to sell you anything. And it is not proper to accept gifts of money from strangers."

"True," said Forever-Mountain. "I will now ask your 69 mother's and grandmother's permission to marry you. I want to be one of the family."

"Oh! I'll get a wedding dress ready!" said Maru-me. 70

The mother and grandmother pretended to consider very 71 seriously, but they quickly agreed.

Next morning Forever-Mountain tied his hair up in the top- 72 knot that all Japanese wrestlers wear, and got ready to leave. He thanked Maru-me and her mother and bowed very low to the grandmother, since she was the oldest and had been a fine wrestling partner.

Then he picked up the cow in his arms and trudged up the 73
mountain. When he reached the top, he slung the cow over one
shoulder and waved good-by to Maru-me.

At the first town he came to, Forever-Mountain sold the cow. 74
She brought a good price because she was unusually fat from
never having worked in her life. With the money, he bought the
heaviest silken belt he could find.

When he reached the palace grounds, many of the other 75
wrestlers were already there, sitting about, eating enormous
bowls of rice, comparing one another's weight and telling stories. They paid little attention to Forever-Mountain, except to
wonder why he had arrived so late this year. Some of them
noticed that he had grown very quiet and took no part at all in
their boasting.

All the ladies and gentlemen of the court were waiting in a 76
special courtyard for the wrestling to begin. They wore many
robes, one on top of another, heavy with embroidery and gold
cloth, and sweat ran down their faces and froze in the winter
afternoon. The gentlemen had long swords so weighted with
gold and precious stones that they could never have used them,
even if they had known how. The court ladies, with their long
black hair hanging down behind, had their faces painted dead
white, which made them look frightened. They had pulled out
their real eyebrows and painted new ones high above the place
where eyebrows are supposed to be, and this made them all look
as though they were very surprised at something.

Behind a screen sat the Emperor—by himself, because he 77
was too noble for ordinary people to look at. He was a lonely old
man with a kind, tired face. He hoped the wrestling would end
quickly so that he could go to his room and write poems.

The first two wrestlers chosen to fight were Forever-Moun- 78
tain and a wrestler who was said to have the biggest stomach in
the country. He and Forever-Mountain both threw some salt
into the ring. It was understood that this drove away evil
spirits.

Then the other wrestler, moving his stomach somewhat out 79
of the way, raised his foot and brought it down with a fearful

stamp. He glared fiercely at Forever-Mountain as if to say, "Now *you* stamp, you poor frightened man!"

Forever-Mountain raised his foot. He brought it down.   80

There was a sound like thunder, the earth shook, and the   81
other wrestler bounced into the air and out of the ring, as gracefully as any soap bubble.

He picked himself up and bowed to the Emperor's screen.   82

"The earth-god is angry. Possibly there is something the matter   83
with the salt," he said. "I do not think I shall wrestle this season." And he walked out, looking very suspiciously over one shoulder at Forever-Mountain.

Five other wrestlers then and there decided that they were   84
not wrestling this season, either. They all looked annoyed with Forever-Mountain.

From then on, Forever-Mountain brought his foot down   85
lightly. As each wrestler came into the ring, he picked him up very gently, carried him out, and placed him before the Emperor's screen, bowing most courteously every time.

The court ladies' eyebrows went up even higher. The gentle-   86
men looked disturbed and a little afraid. They loved to see fierce, strong men tugging and grunting at each other, but Forever-Mountain was a little too much for them. Only the Emperor was happy behind his screen, for now, with the wrestling over so quickly, he would have that much more time to write his poems. He ordered all the prize money handed over to Forever-Mountain.

"But," he said, "you had better not wrestle any more." He   87
stuck a finger through his screen and waggled it at the other wrestlers, who were sitting on the ground weeping with disappointment like great fat babies.

Forever-Mountain promised not to wrestle any more. Every-   88
body looked relieved. The wrestlers sitting on the ground almost smiled.

"I think I shall become a farmer," Forever-Mountain said,   89
and left at once to go back to Maru-me.

Maru-me was waiting for him. When she saw him coming,   90
she ran down the mountain, picked him up, together with the

heavy bags of prize money, and carried him halfway up the mountainside. Then she giggled and put him down. The rest of the way she let him carry her.

Forever-Mountain kept his promise to the Emperor and 91 never fought in public again. His name was forgotten in the capital. But up in the mountains, sometimes, the earth shakes and rumbles, and they say that is Forever-Mountain and Maru-me's grandmother practicing wrestling in the hidden valley.

 Focusing on the Story

1 Where is Forever-Mountain, the famous wrestler, going one fine autumn day?

2 At the beginning of the story, Forever-Mountain says of himself, "I'm a fine, brave man and far too modest to ever say so . . . ." What is ironic about this statement? Is he really modest?

3 Who does he meet as he is "passing above a river bank"?

4 Who are the women that Forever-Mountain meets at the simple farmhouse?

5 Why don't the three women boast about their strength? Is their strength physical only? What must Forever-Mountain do to become stronger?

 Interpreting and Evaluating

1 While pulling the wrestler up the mountain path, Maru-me says, "You'll win or else you'll lose, and you won't be too badly hurt either way." What does she mean by this statement?

2 While he is with the three women in the valley, he grows stronger and stronger, yet he isn't aware of it. Why isn't he so aware of his strength now?

3 Why doesn't Forever-Mountain take part in the other wrestlers' boasting before the wrestling contest at the Imperial Court begins? What has he learned from the three women?

4 At the end of the story, Forever-Mountain promises to forget about wrestling and decides to become a farmer. How can he make this promise so easily now? How has his attitude changed?

5   After the wrestling is over, the other wrestlers are "sitting on the ground weeping with disappointment like great fat babies." How is their reaction similar to Forever-Mountain's after Maru-me has hurt his hand? What has Forever-Mountain taught the other wrestlers?

6   Humor often depends on the unexpected. What are some unexpected situations that are funny in the story?

7   What does this story reveal about Japanese society? What qualities do the Japanese admire? What qualities do they dislike?

 An Idea for Writing and Further Discussion

Humorous stories are often based on unusual characters that solve problems in unexpected and ridiculous ways. Write a humorous story of your own. Begin by choosing a problem and think of a ridiculous solution. The setting may be real or imaginary. Tell the events in chronological order.

Race, Culture, and Identity

A Boy with His Hat over His Crotch

Gish Jen

 Something to Think About

What is it like to come to this country as a foreign student? What is it like to go to another country to live and study? What problems might arise? How could misunderstandings occur?

 Words to Keep in Mind

orotund *(1)* pompous; self-important
dimpled *(1)* with small indentations or impressions as from smiling
placid *(1)* peaceful; unmoving
waxing and waning *(1)* increasing and decreasing in intensity
burial mound *(19)* pile of earth to form a rounded hill over a grave site
Confucius *(19)* Chinese philosopher, ca. 500 B.C., whose teachings became the basis for one of China's major religions
sanguine *(22)* confident; hopeful
dispensed with *(22)* got along without
puckered *(22)* contracted

carnivorous *(34)* meat-eating
crescendo *(52)* gradual increase of intensity of music
permeable *(42)* porous; easy to pass through
shui jiao *(43)* making dumplings (Mandarin Chinese)

P icture him. Young, orotund. Longish hair managed with 1
grease. A new, light gray, too dressy, double-breasted
suit made him look even shorter than his five feet three and
three-quarter inches. Otherwise he was himself—large-faced,
dimpled, with eyebrows that rode nervously up and up, away
from his flat, wide, placid nose. He had small teeth set in vast
expanses of gum; those round ears; and delicate, almost maid-
enly skin that tended to flush and pale with the waxing and
waning of his digestive problems. Everywhere he went, he carried a Panama hat with him, though he never put it on, and it
was always in his way; he seemed to have picked up an idea
about gentlemen, or hats—something—that was proving hard
to let go.

In sum, he was a doll, and the Foreign Student Affairs secre- 2
tary, though she loathed her job, loathed her boss, loathed *working*, liked him.

"Name?" he repeated, or rather "nem," which he knew to be 3
wrong. He turned red, thinking of his trouble with long a's, th's,
l's, consonants at the ends of words. Was it beneath a scholar to
hate the alphabet? Anyway, he did.

"Naaame," she said, writing it down. She'd seen this before, 4
foreign students who could read and write and speak a little, but
who just couldn't get the conversation. N-A-M-E.

"Name Y. F. Chang." (His surname as he pronounced it then 5
sounded like the beginning of *angst*; it would be years before he
was used to hearing Chang rhyme with *twang*.)

"Eng-lish-name," said Cammy. E-N-G-L-I-S-H-N-A-M-E. 6

"I Chin-ese," he said, and was about to explain that Y. F. 7
were his initials when she laughed.

"Eng-lish-name," she said again. 8

"What you laughing?" 9

Later he realized this to be a very daring thing to ask, that he 10
never would have asked a Chinese girl why she was laughing.
But then, a Chinese girl never would have been laughing, not
like that. Not a nice Chinese girl, anyway. What a country he
was in!

"I'm laughing at you." Her voice rang, playful yet deeper 11
than he would have expected. She smelled of perfume. He could
not begin to guess her age. "At *you!*"

"Me?" With mock offense, he drew his chin back. 12

"You," she said again. "Me?" "You." "Me?" They were jok- 13
ing! In English! *Shuo de chu*—he spoke, and the words came out!
Ting de dong—he listened and understood!

"English name," she said again, finally. She showed him her 14
typewriter, the form she had to fill out.

"No English name." How to say initials? He was sorry to 15
disappoint her. Then he brightened. "You give me."

"*I*-give-you-a-name?" 16

"Sure. You give." There was something about speaking 17
English that carried him away.

"I'll-hang-onto-this-form-overnight," she tried to tell him. 18
"That - way - you - find - a - name - you - like - better - you - can -
tell - me - tomorrow."

Too much, he didn't get it. Anyway, he waited, staring— 19
exercising the outsider's privilege, to be rude. How colorful she
was! Orange hair, pink face, blue eyes. Red nails. Green dress.
And under the dress, breasts large and solid as earthworks.
He thought of the burial mounds that dotted the Chinese
countryside—the small mounds for nobodies, the big mounds
for big shots. This woman put him in mind of the biggest
mound he had ever seen: in Shandong, that was, Confucius's
grave.

Meanwhile, she ran through her ex-beaux. Robert? Eugene? 20
Norman? She toyed with a stray curl. Fred? John? Steve? Ken?

"Ralph," she said finally. She wrote it down. R-A-L-P-H. "Do you like it?"

"Sure!" He beamed.   21

Walking home, though, *Ralph* was less sanguine. Had he 22
been too hasty? He did this, he knew; he dispensed with things,
trying to be like other people—decisive, practical—only to discover he'd overdone it. His stomach puckered with anxiety. And
sure enough, when he asked around later he found that the
other Chinese students (there were five of them in the master's
degree program) had all stuck with their initials, or picked
names for themselves, carefully, or else had wise people help
them.

"Ralph," said smooth-faced Old Chao (Old Something-or- 23
another being what younger classmates called older classmates,
who in turn called them Little Something-or-another). He
looked it up in a book he had. "Means *wolf*," he said, then looked
that up in a dictionary. "*A kind of dog*," he translated.

A kind of dog, thought Ralph.   24

For himself, Old Chao had Henry, which turned out to be the 25
name of at least eight kings. "*My father picked it for me*," he said.

It would have been better if Ralph sounded a bit more like 26
Yifeng; in the art of picking English names (which everyone
seemed to know except him), that was considered desirable. But
so what? And who cared what it meant? Ralph decided that
what was on the form didn't matter. He was a man with a mission; what mattered was that he register for the right courses,
that he attend the right classes, that he buy the right books. All
of this proved more difficult than he'd anticipated. He discovered, for instance, that he wasn't on the class list for two of his
courses, and that for one of them, enrollment was already
closed. To address these problems, he did what he did when his
tuition didn't arrive, and when his other two classes turned out
to meet at the same time: he found his way to the Foreign Student Affairs Office, where gaily colored Cammy would help
him.

Ralph had noticed by then that she was pretty, or figured she 27
must be, as about half the men with affairs to discuss with her

didn't seem to be foreign students. ("Fan club," explained Old Chao, idiom book in hand.) With her big barbarian frame and long nose and hairy forearms, though, she just wasn't Ralph's type (the hair bothered him especially—like a monkey's, he thought); and anyway, he was too exhausted to be thinking about such things—having come, he belatedly realized, to the complete other side of the world. Mile after mile, he'd travelled, *li* after *li*, by boat and by train, only to have to get himself going. His degree, his degree!

And so to Cammy he was grateful, nothing more.   28

"Tank you," he said. "Tank you." One day he helped fix her   29
pencil sharpener, and when she said "Tank *you*," he answered, "Sure!" And after that, whenever he said "Tank you," she answered "Sure!" too. This came with a wink, and a kind of sideways look that made Ralph's pants bulge—lucky thing he was still carrying that hat around.

Did he confuse this phenomenon with love? Not yet. He   30
stacked paper for Cammy. He taught her to say thank you in Chinese. "Shay shay!" she said now, whenever she saw him, whether she had reason to thank him or not. "Shay shay shay shay!" Ralph tried to get her to speak more correctly. "Sh-yeh," he told her. "Sh-yeh, sh-yeh." He concentrated on getting his own pronunciation right, not wanting to pass on to her his Shanghainese hiss. So little of what he knew counted here; he offered what he could on a kind of tray. "Isn't that what I said?" she asked. "Shay shay?" And before he'd had a chance to say yes or no, she was back to "Shay shay shay shay!" again, with such exuberance, Ralph didn't have the heart to do anything but nod. "Good!"

"You know, one of these days I'm going to study Chinese,"   31
said Cammy. "Chinese or French. Or else ballet, I've always loved ballet."

"Ah," said Ralph (this being the sort of thing he was begin-   32
ning to understand he should say instead of "Wha?" when there was something he couldn't catch).

More favors, innocent enough—packages to the mailbox,   33
expeditious disposal of a bumblebee. And, of course, help with her boss, Mr. Fitt.

Now Mr. Fitt was a grim man, an enforcer, with a small, sneer-   34
ing mouth; in another life he might have been a carnivorous fish.
In this life, he carried a rolled-up newspaper in his thick hand like
a bat he meant to use on someone. When Ralph wandered onto
the scene, Mr. Fitt was tapping that bat on his thigh; his other hand
was all five hairy fingers on Cammy's neat desk.

"But I w-was here. At one on th-the b-b-button." The sound   35
of Cammy choked up made Ralph's throat catch. "Wasn't I,
Ralph? Wasn't I?"

Ralph gave solemn testimony. Mr. Fitt straightened up, glar-   36
ing. Cammy was all shay shays. "Tell me how to say it again,"
she said. "I know I don't say it right. I don't do anything right."

"No, no, you pronounce very good."   37

"No I don't. You say it again, the right way."   38

Ralph hesitated. "Shay shay."   39

"Shay shay." She lit up. "Shay shay! You mean, I *am* saying it   40
right? Shay shay?"

Ralph nodded, beamed, situated his hat.   41

More and more now, he was beginning to know what was   42
what. He was lonely still, but it was only a mist, a weather front
that passed through him when he was alone, a feeling of having
turned too permeable. When he was working, he was fine. And
having launched into his work, he did not go to the Foreign Student Affairs Office anymore, but rather to the stone-stepped
library, where he studied and studied at the endless oak tables;
or else to the kitchen at the end of the hall in his rooming house
on 123rd Street. There, on the blackboard by the stove, he puzzled out problems with his classmates. Between equations, they
marvelled that their tests would be scored to the whole point,
instead of to five decimal places. Was it fair? Who knew? This
was America. They forged on, mostly speaking Mandarin, saving their English for impersonations of certain professors.

The kitchen was where Ralph spent his free time too, learn-   43
ing to cook. He could make three dishes now—boiled rice, egg
rice, and fried eggs. Having thrown several successful *shui jiao*-
making parties, his classmates were organizing a cooperative

cooking program, and Ralph was practicing up, to be sure he'd be able to participate. Other developments: he'd discovered supper for a dollar at General Lee's, and also banana splits with extra nuts and marshmallow sauce (the specialty of the luncheonette down the street). Also, he'd bought a lamp for his room, from the secondhand store next to the grocery he used to go to. Already he had a history in America. Now he went to a new, cheaper grocery, even though the first grocer was friendlier than the second, and had been so nice as to count his change out slowly, one coin at a time.

From his doorway, the first grocer scowled at him.   44

The problem sets got harder.   45

His lamp turned out to have a short in it.   46

His problem sets started to come back red.   47

More red.   48

Who had ever thought the rice barrel could become an engineer?   49

New York lost its gleam. He drifted through its streets as if through an exhausted, dusty land, no detail of which had changed in a thousand years.   50

Then he remembered a form he was supposed to have handed in (some form, he had always been bad at that sort of thing) and, stopping into the Foreign Student Affairs Office, discovered Cammy arguing once again with Mr. Fitt. What a bully that man was! His whole long belly overhung Cammy's desk; he had his arms spread and bent, his fingers on her blotter. Cammy was holding her hands over her ears.   51

Ralph's heart rumbled like a Peking Opera drum; it was the crescendo before—*crash of the cymbals!*—a hero appeared.   52

 Focusing on the Story

1   Describe Yifeng Chang as he arrives at the Foreign Student Affairs Office.

2   Describe Cammy, the Foreign Student Affairs Office secretary, as Yifeng Chang sees her. What are some things Cammy does for Yifeng

Chang? How does she make him feel? What are some things Yifeng does for Cammy? Why can Yifeng not "begin to guess her age"? How does Cammy differ from young Chinese women?

3 What does Yifeng's American name Ralph mean? How does Yifeng feel about his new name when he discovers its meaning?

4 Yifeng accepts his new name rather quickly, without thinking it over. How does he later justify his rash behavior?

5 What is Yifeng or Ralph's "mission" in the United States? Why can't he accomplish this mission in China?

 Interpreting and Evaluating

1 It has been customary for new immigrants to this country to anglicize their names for ease of pronunciation and spelling by native speakers of English. How much of your identity does your name represent? How would you feel if someone decided to change your name by whim?

2 When Yifeng realizes that he has accepted his new name too readily, he rationalizes that his hasty move is not important. What does his behavior say about his character?

3 Ralph studies at the library, finds where the best bargains are, and learns to cook. What does all this, as well as his other actions, say about Ralph's ability to adapt? Will he ultimately succeed? Explain.

4 At the end of the story, Ralph comes to Cammy's rescue again—"a hero appeared." Based on evidence in the story, what predictions can you make about Cammy and Ralph's future relationship? Could their relationship develop into a romantic one? Explain.

5 How may a marriage between people from different cultures be more difficult than a marriage between people from similar backgrounds?

 Ideas for Writing and Further Discussion

1 What are some causes of misunderstandings between people from different cultures? Write an essay in which you explore several causes of misunderstandings between people from different cultures.

Suggested *thesis*: two or three such causes.

Each *body paragraph* should discuss one cause. You may suggest a solution to the problem in your conclusion.

2   Although Yifeng, or Ralph, has many obstacles to overcome, most people would probably agree that he has what it takes to succeed in this country. Analyze Ralph's character. What in his character will help him succeed? Write an essay in which you discuss several of Ralph's qualities that will contribute to his success in his new country.

Suggested *thesis*: three or four such qualities.

Each *body paragraph* should explore one quality and give examples from the story to illustrate the quality and show how possessing such a quality will lead to success. Or one body paragraph may discuss some obstacles Yifeng, or Ralph, has to overcome; the remaining body paragraphs should explore his positive qualities.

By Any Other Name

Santha Rama Rau

About the Author

Santha Rama Rau was born in India in 1923, but received her education in the West. Because of her familiarity with both Eastern and Western points of view, her books are highly regarded for their insight. This selection is taken from her autobiography, *Gifts of Passage.*

 Something to Think About

India was ruled by Great Britain from the 1700s to 1947. What effects may a ruling country have on a local culture? What kinds of stereotypes may be formed? What effects of Great Britain's rule over the American Colonies can you see today in your own life?

 Words to Keep in Mind

precarious *(3)* not secure; unstable

baffled *(3)* frustrated; confused

insular *(6)* isolated; separated

Lord Krishna *(6)* ancient Hindu god whose childhood pranks provide popular stories for Indian children even today

veranda *(7)* porch

kohl *(9)* special coal used as eye makeup in India and many other countries

palpitating *(15)* trembling, throbbing

incomprehensible *(15)* impossible to understand

chapatties *(16)* whole-grain bread made without baking powder or yeast

ayah *(18)* Indian maid (literally *grandmother*)

sedately *(22)* calmly

tonga *(34)* a light two-wheeled wagon common in India

peevishness *(34)* irritation

A t the Anglo-Indian day school in Zorinabad to which my 1
sister and I were sent when she was eight and I was five
and a half, they changed our names. On the first day of school, a
hot, windless morning of a north Indian September, we stood in
the headmistress's study and she said, "Now you're the *new*
girls. What are your names?"

My sister answered for us. "I am Premila, and she"—nod- 2
ding in my direction—"is Santha."

The headmistress had been in India, I suppose, fifteen years 3
or so, but she still smiled her helpless inability to cope with
Indian names. Her rimless half-glasses glittered, and the precarious bun on the top of her head trembled as she shook her head.
"Oh, my dears, those are much too hard for me. Suppose we
give you pretty English names. Wouldn't that be more jolly?
Let's see, now—Pamela for you, I think." She shrugged in a baffled way at my sister. "That's as close as I can get. And for *you*,"
she said to me, "how about Cynthia? Isn't that nice?"

My sister was always less easily intimidated than I was, and 4
while she kept a stubborn silence, I said, "Thank you," in a very
tiny voice.

We had been sent to that school because my father, among 5
his responsibilities as an officer of the civil service, had a tour of

duty to perform in the villages around that steamy little provincial town, where he had his headquarters at that time. He used to make his shorter inspection tours on horseback, and a week before, in the stale heat of a typically postmonsoon day, we had waved good-by to him and a little procession—an assistant, a secretary, two bearers, and the man to look after the bedding rolls and luggage. They rode away through our large garden, still bright green from the rains, and we turned back into the twilight of the house and the sound of fans whispering in every room.

Up to then, my mother had refused to send Premila to school 6 in the British-run establishments of that time, because, she used to say, "you can bury a dog's tail for seven years and it still comes out curly, and you can take a Britisher away from his home for a lifetime and he still remains insular." The examinations and degrees from entirely Indian schools were not, in those days, considered valid. In my case, the question had never come up, and probably never would have come up if Mother's extraordinary good health had not broken down. For the first time in my life, she was not able to continue the lessons she had been giving us every morning. So our Hindi books were put away, the stories of the Lord Krishna as a little boy were left in mid-air, and we were sent to the Anglo-Indian school.

That first day at school is still, when I think of it, a remark- 7 able one. At that age, if one's name is changed, one develops a curious form of dual personality. I remember having a certain detached and disbelieving concern in the actions of "Cynthia," but certainly no responsibility. Accordingly, I followed the thin, erect back of the headmistress down the veranda to my classroom feeling, at most, a passing interest in what was going to happen to me in this strange, new atmosphere of School.

The building was Indian in design, with wide verandas 8 opening into a central courtyard, but Indian verandas are usually whitewashed, with stone floors. These, in the tradition of British schools, were painted dark brown and had matting on the floors. It gave a feeling of extra intensity to the heat.

I suppose there were about a dozen Indian children in the   9
school—which contained perhaps forty children in all—and four
of them were in my class. They were all sitting at the back of the
room, and I went to join them. I sat next to a small solemn girl
who didn't smile at me. She had long, glossy-black braids and
wore a cotton dress, but she still kept on her Indian jewelry—a
gold chain around her neck, thin gold bracelets, and tiny ruby
studs in her ears. Like most Indian children, she had a rim of
black kohl around her eyes. The cotton dress should have looked
strange, but all I could think of was that I should ask my mother
if I couldn't wear a dress to school, too, instead of my Indian
clothes.

I can't remember too much about the proceedings in class   10
that day, except for the beginning. The teacher pointed to me
and asked me to stand up. "Now, dear, tell the class your name."

I said nothing.   11

"Come along," she said, frowning slightly. "What's your   12
name, dear?"

"I don't know," I said, finally.   13

The English children in the front of the class—there were   14
about eight or ten of them—giggled and twisted around in their
chairs to look at me. I sat down quickly and opened my eyes
very wide, hoping in that way to dry them off. The little girl with
the braids put out her hand and very lightly touched my arm.
She still didn't smile.

Most of that morning I was rather bored. I looked briefly at   15
the children's drawings pinned to the wall, and then concentrated on a lizard clinging to the ledge of the high, barred window behind the teacher's head. Occasionally it would shoot out
its long yellow tongue for a fly, and then it would rest, with its
eyes closed and its belly palpitating, as though it were swallow-
ing several times quickly. The lessons were mostly concerned
with reading and writing and simple numbers—things that my
mother had already taught me—and I paid very little attention.
The teacher wrote on the easel blackboard words like "bat" and
"cat," which seemed babyish to me; only "apple" was new and
incomprehensible.

When it was time for the lunch recess, I followed the girl 16
with braids out onto the veranda. There the children from the
other classes were assembled. I saw Premila at once and ran over
to her, as she had charge of our lunchbox. The children were all
opening packages and sitting down to eat sandwiches. Premila
and I were the only ones who had Indian food—thin wheat chapatties, some vegetable curry, and a bottle of buttermilk. Premila
thrust half of it into my hand and whispered fiercely that I
should go and sit with my class, because that was what the others seemed to be doing.

The enormous black eyes of the little Indian girl from my 17
class looked at my food longingly, so I offered her some. But she
only shook her head and plowed her way solemnly through her
sandwiches.

I was very sleepy after lunch, because at home we always 18
took a siesta. It was usually a pleasant time of day, with the bedroom darkened against the harsh afternoon sun, the drifting off
into sleep with the sound of Mother's voice reading a story in
one's mind, and, finally, the shrill, fussy voice of the ayah wak-
ing one for tea.

At school, we rested for a short time on low, folding cots on 19
the veranda, and then we were expected to play games. During
the hot part of the afternoon we played indoors, and after the
shadows had begun to lengthen and the slight breeze of the
evening had come up we moved outside to the wide courtyard.

I had never really grasped the system of competitive games. 20
At home, whenever we played tag or guessing games, I was
always allowed to "win"—"because," Mother used to tell Premila, "she is the youngest, and we have to allow for that." I had
often heard her say it, and it seemed quite reasonable to me, but
the result was that I had no clear idea of what "winning" meant.

When we played twos-and-threes that afternoon at school, in 21
accordance with my training, I let one of the small English boys
catch me, but was naturally rather puzzled when the other children did not return the courtesy. I ran about for what seemed
like hours without ever catching anyone, until it was time for
school to close. Much later I learned that my attitude was called

"not being a good sport," and I stopped allowing myself to be caught, but it was not for years that I really learned the spirit of the thing.

When I saw our car come up to the school gate, I broke away   22
from my classmates and rushed toward it yelling, "Ayah! Ayah!" It seemed like an eternity since I had seen her that morning—a wizened, affectionate figure in her white cotton sari, giving me dozens of urgent and useless instructions on how to be a good girl at school. Premila followed more sedately, and she told me on the way home never to do that again in front of the other children.

When we got home we went straight to Mother's high, white   23
room to have tea with her, and I immediately climbed onto the bed and bounced gently up and down on the springs. Mother asked how we had liked our first day in school. I was so pleased to be home and to have left that peculiar Cynthia behind that I had nothing whatever to say about school, except to ask what "apple" meant. But Premila told Mother about the classes, and added that in her class they had weekly tests to see if they had learned their lessons well.

I asked, "What's a test?"   24

Premila said, "You're too small to have them. You won't   25
have them in your class for donkey's years." She had learned the expression that day and was using it for the first time. We all laughed enormously at her wit. She also told Mother, in an aside, that we should take sandwiches to school the next day. Not, she said, that *she* minded. But they would be simpler for me to handle.

That whole lovely evening I didn't think about school at all. I   26
sprinted barefoot across the lawns with my favorite playmate, the cook's son, to the stream at the end of the garden. We quarreled in our usual way, waded in the tepid water under the lime trees, and waited for the night to bring out the smell of the jasmine. I listened with fascination to his stories of ghosts and demons, until I was too frightened to cross the garden alone in the semidarkness. The ayah found me, shouted at the cook's son, scolded me, hurried me in to supper—it was an entirely usual, wonderful evening.

It was a week later, the day of Premila's first test, that our   27
lives changed rather abruptly. I was sitting at the back of my
class, in my usual inattentive way, only half listening to the
teacher. I had started a rather guarded friendship with the girl
with the braids, whose name turned out to be Nalini (Nancy,
in school). The three other Indian children were already fast
friends. Even at that age it was apparent to all of us that friendship with the English or Anglo-Indian children was out of the
question. Occasionally, during the class, my new friend and I
would draw pictures and show them to each other secretly.

The door opened sharply and Premila marched in. At first,   28
the teacher smiled at her in a kindly and encouraging way and
said, "Now, you're little Cynthia's sister?"

Premila didn't even look at her. She stood with her feet   29
planted firmly apart and her shoulders rigid, and addressed herself directly to me. "Get up," she said. "We're going home."

I didn't know what had happened, but I was aware that it   30
was a crisis of some sort. I rose obediently and started to walk
toward my sister.

"Bring your pencils and your notebook," she said.   31

I went back for them, and together we left the room. The   32
teacher started to say something just as Premila closed the door,
but we didn't wait to hear what it was.

In complete silence we left the school grounds and started to   33
walk home. Then I asked Premila what the matter was. All she
would say was "We're going home for good."

It was a very tiring walk for a child of five and a half, and I   34
dragged along behind Premila with my pencils growing sticky
in my hand. I can still remember looking at the dusty hedges,
and the tangles of thorns in the ditches by the side of the road,
smelling the faint fragrance from the eucalyptus trees and wondering whether we would ever reach home. Occasionally a
horse-drawn tonga passed us, and the women, in their pink or
green silks, stared at Premila and me trudging along on the side
of the road. A few coolies and a line of women carrying baskets
of vegetables on their heads smiled at us. But it was nearing the
hottest time of day, and the road was almost deserted. I walked

more and more slowly, and shouted to Premila, from time to time, "Wait for me!" with increasing peevishness. She spoke to me only once, and that was to tell me to carry my notebook on my head, because of the sun.

When we got to our house the ayah was just taking a tray of 35
lunch into Mother's room. She immediately started a long, worried questioning about what are you children doing back here at this hour of the day.

Mother looked very startled and very concerned, and asked 36
what had happened.

Premila said, "We had our test today, and She made me and 37
the other Indians sit at the back of the room, with a desk between each one."

Mother said, "Why was that, darling?" 38

"She said it was because Indians cheat," Premila added. "So 39
I don't think we should go back to that school."

Mother looked very distant, and was silent a long time. At 40
last she said, "Of course not, darling." She sounded displeased.

We all shared the curry she was having for lunch, and after- 41
ward I was sent off to the beautifully familiar bedroom for my siesta. I could hear Mother and Premila talking through the open door.

Mother said, "Do you suppose she understood all that?" 42

Premila said, "I shouldn't think so. She's a baby." 43

Mother said, "Well, I hope it won't bother her." 44

Of course, they were both wrong. I understood it perfectly, 45
and I remember it all very clearly. But I put it happily away, because it had all happened to a girl called Cynthia, and I never was really particularly interested in her.

 Focusing on the Story

1   What nationality are the two sisters? What nationality are the headmistress and the teachers at the Anglo-Indian school?

2   How did Santha feel about and react to her new name, Cynthia? Why couldn't the teachers remember Indian names? Had the headmistress just recently arrived in the country?

3   What was the economic status of Santha's family? Did they speak English? Give evidence from the story to support your answers.

4   Why did the Indian children have to sit in the back of the classroom? Why was friendship between the Indian and English children "out of the question"?

5   Why did the sisters abruptly leave school after one week? Were they coming back? What did Premila's teacher accuse Indian children of?

 Interpreting and Evaluating

1   How were degrees from Indian schools regarded at that time? What may have been some reasons for this lack of recognition?

2   On the first day of school, Santha, or Cynthia, was bored and didn't seem to pay much attention. Was she a slow learner? Why did she find the word *apple* incomprehensible?

3   Why did Premila, or Pamela, want to take English sandwiches rather than Indian food to school? And why did Santha, or Cynthia, want to wear a dress rather than Indian clothes?

4   When Premila came to take Santha home on their last day at the English school, "she stood with her feet planted firmly apart and shoulders rigid." What can you infer about Premila's feelings from this description?

5   How did the English teachers stereotype the Indians? How did Santha and Premila react to this stereotyping? How may this stereotyping have affected the Indian children's self-esteem in general?

 Ideas for Writing and Further Discussion

1   Santha's short time at the British school in India obviously had a profound effect on her and probably changed her way of thinking for life. Write about a similar experience that has had a profound effect on your way of thinking. Describe what happened, and explain how and why it affected you so deeply.

It's not necessary to write a formal thesis statement in a narrative essay, but you may wish to start with a general statement that expresses an attitude toward the experience.

2   What are some ways to overcome prejudice? Write an essay in which you explore two or three ways to deal with prejudice. Write an introduction that catches the reader's attention.

Suggested *thesis*: two or three ways to deal with prejudice.

Each *body paragraph* should include one specific way to overcome prejudice. Supply several reasons why each suggestion is a good way to deal with prejudice.

Mary

Maya Angelou

About the Author

Maya Angelou, whose real name is Marguerite, was born in Arkansas in 1928. She spent much of her childhood with her grandmother and her brother, Bailey, in Stamps, Arkansas. At the age of eight, while staying with her mother in St. Louis, she was raped by her mother's boyfriend, Mr. Freeman, referred to in this story. For several years afterward, she refused to speak to anyone but her brother. A poet, Maya Angelou will long be remembered for the moving reading of her own poem at President Bill Clinton's inauguration.

 Something to Think About

How do you react when someone insults you or talks down to you? Do you talk back? What if he or she is your boss?

 Words to Keep in Mind

ecru *(1)* light tan color

tatting *(1)* making fine lace by looping and knotting cotton or linen thread with a special tatting shuttle

sacheted *(2)* perfumed with small bags of ground flower petals

impish *(3)* like a mischievous child

Cheshire cat *(12)* the grinning cat in *Alice in Wonderland*

Cupid *(12)* Roman god of love, often pictured as a small boy with a bow and arrows

barrenness *(13)* lack of ability to bear children

speckled *(14)* marked with spots

four-o'clocks *(22)* small trumpet-shaped red or white flowers that open in the late afternoon

dilemma *(37)* difficult choice

biddies *(37)* talkative women

N egro girls in small Southern towns, whether poverty- 1
stricken or just munching along on a few of life's neces-
sities, were given as extensive and irrelevant preparations for
adulthood as rich white girls shown in magazines. Admittedly
the training was not the same. While white girls learned to waltz
and sit gracefully with a tea cup balanced on their knees, we
were lagging behind, learning the mid-Victorian values with
very little money to indulge them. (Come and see Edna Lomax
spending the money she made picking cotton on five balls of
ecru tatting thread. Her fingers are bound to snag the work and
she'll have to repeat the stitches time and time again. But she
knows that when she buys the thread.)

We were required to embroider and I had trunkfuls of color- 2
ful dishtowels, pillowcases, runners, and handkerchiefs to my
credit. I mastered the art of crocheting and tatting, and there was
a lifetime's supply of dainty doilies that would never be used in
sacheted dresser drawers. It went without saying that all girls
could iron and wash, but the finer touches around the home, like
setting a table with real silver, baking roasts, and cooking vegetables without meat, had to be learned elsewhere. Usually at
the source of those habits. During my tenth year, a white
woman's kitchen became my finishing school.

Mrs. Viola Cullinan was a plump woman who lived in a 3
three-bedroom house somewhere behind the post office. She
was singularly unattractive until she smiled, and then the lines
around her eyes and mouth which made her look perpetually

From *I Know Why the Caged Bird Sings,* pages 101–108. © 1969 by Maya
Angelou and © renewed 1997. Reprinted by permission of Random
House, Inc.

dirty disappeared, and her face looked like the mask of an impish elf. She usually rested her smile until late afternoon when her women friends dropped in and Miss Glory, the cook, served them cold drinks on the closed-in porch.

The exactness of her house was inhuman. This glass went 4
here and only here. That cup had its place and it was an act of impudent rebellion to place it anywhere else. At twelve o'clock the table was set. At 12:15 Mrs. Cullinan sat down to dinner (whether her husband had arrived or not). At 12:16 Miss Glory brought out the food.

It took me a week to learn the difference between a salad 5
plate, a bread plate, and a dessert plate.

Mrs. Cullinan kept up the tradition of her wealthy parents. 6
She was from Virginia. Miss Glory, who was a descendant of slaves that had worked for the Cullinans, told me her history. She had married beneath her (according to Miss Glory). Her husband's family hadn't had their money very long and what they had "didn't 'mount to much."

As ugly as she was, I thought privately, she was lucky to get 7
a husband above or beneath her station. But Miss Glory wouldn't let me say a thing against her mistress. She was very patient with me, however, over the housework. She explained the dishware, silverware, and servants' bells.

The large round bowl in which soup was served wasn't a 8
soup bowl, it was a tureen. There were goblets, sherbet glasses, ice-cream glasses, wine glasses, green glass coffee cups with matching saucers, and water glasses. I had a glass to drink from, and it sat with Miss Glory's on a separate shelf from the others. Soup spoons, gravy boat, butter knives, salad forks, and carving platter were additions to my vocabulary and in fact almost represented a new language. I was fascinated with the novelty, with the fluttering Mrs. Cullinan and her Alice-in-Wonderland house.

Her husband remains, in my memory, undefined. I lumped 9
him with all the other white men that I had ever seen and tried not to see.

On our way home one evening, Miss Glory told me that Mrs. 10
Cullinan couldn't have children. She said that she was too delicate-boned. It was hard to imagine bones at all under those

layers of fat. Miss Glory went on to say that the doctor had taken out all her lady organs. I reasoned that a pig's organs included the lungs, heart, and liver, so if Mrs. Cullinan was walking around without those essentials, it explained why she drank alcohol out of unmarked bottles. She was keeping herself embalmed.

When I spoke to Bailey about it, he agreed that I was right, 11 but he also informed me that Mr. Cullinan had two daughters by a colored lady and that I knew them very well. He added that the girls were the spitting image of their father. I was unable to remember what he looked like, although I had just left him a few hours before, but I thought of the Coleman girls. They were very light-skinned and certainly didn't look very much like their mother (no one ever mentioned Mr. Coleman).

My pity for Mrs. Cullinan preceded me the next morning 12 like the Cheshire cat's smile. Those girls, who could have been her daughters, were beautiful. They didn't have to straighten their hair. Even when they were caught in the rain, their braids still hung down straight like tamed snakes. Their mouths were pouty little Cupid's bows. Mrs. Cullinan didn't know what she missed. Or maybe she did. Poor Mrs. Cullinan.

For weeks after, I arrived early, left late, and tried very hard 13 to make up for her barrenness. If she had had her own children, she wouldn't have had to ask me to run a thousand errands from her back door to the back door of her friends. Poor old Mrs. Cullinan.

Then one evening Miss Glory told me to serve the ladies on 14 the porch. After I set the tray down and turned toward the kitchen, one of the women asked, "What's your name, girl?" It was the speckled-faced one. Mrs. Cullinan said, "She doesn't talk much. Her name's Margaret."

"Is she dumb?" 15

"No. As I understand it, she can talk when she wants to but 16 she's usually quiet as a little mouse. Aren't you, Margaret?"

I smiled at her. Poor thing. No organs and couldn't even pro- 17 nounce my name correctly.

"She's a sweet little thing, though." 18

"Well, that may be, but the name's too long. I'd never bother   19
myself. I'd call her Mary if I was you."

I fumed into the kitchen. That horrible woman would never   20
have the chance to call me Mary because if I was starving I'd
never work for her. I decided I wouldn't pee on her if her heart
was on fire. Giggles drifted in off the porch and into
Miss Glory's pots. I wondered what they could be laughing
about.

Whitefolks were so strange. Could they be talking about   21
me? Everybody knew that they stuck together better than the
Negroes did. It was possible that Mrs. Cullinan had friends in
St. Louis who heard about a girl from Stamps being in court and
wrote to tell her. Maybe she knew about Mr. Freeman.

My lunch was in my mouth a second time and I went out-   22
side and relieved myself on the bed of four-o'clocks. Miss Glory
thought I might be coming down with something and told me to
go on home, that Momma would give me some herb tea, and
she'd explain to her mistress.

I realized how foolish I was being before I reached the pond.   23
Of course Mrs. Cullinan didn't know. Otherwise she wouldn't
have given me the two nice dresses that Momma cut down,
and she certainly wouldn't have called me a "sweet little
thing." My stomach felt fine, and I didn't mention anything to
Momma.

That evening I decided to write a poem on being white, fat,   24
old, and without children. It was going to be a tragic ballad. I
would have to watch her carefully to capture the essence of her
loneliness and pain.

The very next day, she called me by the wrong name. Miss   25
Glory and I were washing up the lunch dishes when Mrs. Cullinan came to the doorway. "Mary?"

Miss Glory asked, "Who?"   26

Mrs. Cullinan, sagging a little, knew and I knew. "I want   27
Mary to go down to Mrs. Randall's and take her some soup.
She's not been feeling well for a few days."

Miss Glory's face was a wonder to see. "You mean Margaret,   28
ma'am. Her name's Margaret."

"'That's too long. She's Mary from now on. Heat that soup   29
from last night and put it in the china tureen and, Mary, I want
you to carry it carefully."

Every person I knew had a hellish horror of being "called   30
out of his own name." It was a dangerous practice to call a
Negro anything that could be loosely construed as insulting
because of the centuries of their having been called niggers, jigs,
dinges, blackbirds, crows, boots, and spooks.

Miss Glory had a fleeting second of feeling sorry for me.   31
Then as she handed me the hot tureen she said, "Don't mind,
don't pay that no mind. Sticks and stones may break your bones,
but words . . . You know, I been working for her for twenty
years."

She held the back door open for me. "Twenty years. I wasn't   32
much older than you. My name used to be Hallelujah. That's
what Ma named me, but my mistress give me 'Glory,' and it
stuck. I likes it better too."

I was in the little path that ran behind the houses when Miss   33
Glory shouted, "It's shorter too."

For a few seconds it was a tossup over whether I would   34
laugh (imagine being named Hallelujah) or cry (imagine letting
some white woman rename you for her convenience). My anger
saved me from either outburst. I had to quit the job, but the
problem was going to be how to do it. Momma wouldn't allow
me to quit for just any reason.

"She's a peach. That woman is a real peach." Mrs. Randall's   35
maid was talking as she took the soup from me, and I wondered
what her name used to be and what she answered to now.

For a week I looked into Mrs. Cullinan's face as she called   36
me Mary. She ignored my coming late and leaving early. Miss
Glory was a little annoyed because I had begun to leave egg
yolk on the dishes and wasn't putting much heart in polishing
the silver. I hoped that she would complain to our boss, but she
didn't.

Then Bailey solved my dilemma. He had me describe the   37
contents of the cupboard and the particular plates she liked best.
Her favorite piece was a casserole shaped like a fish and the
green glass coffee cups. I kept his instructions in mind, so on the

next day when Miss Glory was hanging out clothes and I had again been told to serve the old biddies on the porch, I dropped the empty serving tray. When I heard Mrs. Cullinan scream, "Mary!" I picked up the casserole and two of the green glass cups in readiness. As she rounded the kitchen door I let them fall on the tiled floor.

I could never absolutely describe to Bailey what happened next, because each time I got to the part where she fell on the floor and screwed up her ugly face to cry, we burst out laughing. She actually wobbled around on the floor and picked up shards of the cups and cried, "Oh, Momma. Oh, dear Gawd. It's Momma's china from Virginia. Oh, Momma, I sorry." 30

Miss Glory came running in from the yard and the women from the porch crowded around. Miss Glory was almost as broken up as her mistress. "You mean to say she broke our Virginia dishes? What we gone do?" 39

Mrs. Cullinan cried louder, "That clumsy nigger. Clumsy little black nigger." 40

Old speckled-face leaned down and asked, "Who did it, Viola? Was it Mary? Who did it?" 41

Everything was happening so fast I can't remember whether her action preceded her words, but I know that Mrs. Cullinan said, "Her name's Margaret, goddamn it, her name's Margaret!" And she threw a wedge of the broken plate at me. It could have been the hysteria which put her aim off, but the flying crockery caught Miss Glory right over her ear and she started screaming. 42

I left the front door wide open so all the neighbors could hear. 43

Mrs. Cullinan was right about one thing. My name wasn't Mary. 44

 Focusing on the Story

1   List some tasks that African-American girls had to learn in preparation for adulthood in the 1930s and 1940s, the time the story takes place. How were they similar to the tasks that white girls have to master? How were they different?

2   Describe Mrs. Viola Cullinan, the white woman in whose service Margaret, or Marguerite, learned "the finer touches around the home." How did Margaret feel about working in the house at first?

3   In paragraph 4, the author writes that "the exactness of [Mrs. Viola Cullinan's] house was inhuman." What does this mean?

4   What was Miss Glory's real name? Why did Mrs. Cullinan change it? Why did she suddenly start to call Margaret "Mary"? How did Margaret feel about working for Mrs. Cullinan after being called "Mary"?

5   What did Margaret hope to achieve by breaking the casserole and the green glass coffee cups?

Interpreting and Evaluating

1   In paragraph 1, the author writes that "girls in small Southern towns . . . were given . . . irrelevant preparations for adulthood." Such preparations are in fact common in many cultures. Why may such customs be maintained? How may traditions be both a hindrance to progress and something to be cherished?

2   While staying with her mother in St. Louis, Maya Angelou was raped by her mother's boyfriend, Mr. Freeman. In paragraphs 21, 22, and 23, her thoughts focus on that incident. How does she feel about it? Why did she feel that if Mrs. Cullinan had known about it, she wouldn't have given her "the nice dresses" nor called her a "sweet little thing"?

3   Why is the author, who today is known by the name "Maya," so upset about being called "Mary" rather than Margaret? After all, calling people by their shorter nicknames is a common practice in the United States. What is different in this situation? How would you have handled it if you had been in Margaret's place?

4   How would you characterize Margaret? How is she different from Miss Glory? Use examples from the story to illustrate your point.

5   The tone of a story reflects the author's attitude to the subject matter. How would you describe the tone of this story? Point out specific words and phrases the author has chosen to convey this tone.

Ideas for Writing and Further Discussion

1   Do you remember your first job? Write two or three paragraphs describing your first job. How old were you? What was your employer like? What did you have to do? How much money did you make? How did it make you feel?

2 Does your family maintain a unique tradition? Write a paragraph or two describing a special tradition in your family. How do you feel about it?

3 Mrs. Viola Cullinan is driven by her daily routine: lunch is served at 12:16 every day; her lady friends drop in every afternoon. Write three or four paragraphs describing the routine in your own household.

It's not necessary to write a formal thesis statement in a narrative essay, but you may wish to start with a general statement that expresses an attitude toward the experience.

Victims of Armed Conflict

Children
and Old Folk

Ivan Cankar

About the Author

Ivan Cankar was born in 1876 in Slovenia, the northernmost republic
in former Yugoslavia. In addition to being a prolific writer of novels,
plays, and short stories, he was a political speaker who defended the
poor and criticized those who exploited them. He was imprisoned for
his views and criticism of the government and died in 1918.

 Something to Think About

A small child once asked, "How can soldiers killing each other bring
peace?" Is this a childish question? How do children perceive war?

 Words to Keep in Mind

enthralled *(2)* fascinated

beauteous *(2)* poetic form for the word *beautiful*

introspective *(3)* looking within to examine one's own thoughts and
feelings

incomprehensible *(4)* impossible to understand

clamorous *(4)* noisy

wherefore *(5)* why

whence *(5)* from where

apparition *(5)* ghost

ponderous *(5)* dull, tiresome

lapsed into *(8)* fell into
admonished *(10)* warned
wayfarer *(11)* traveler
retorted *(24)* answered sharply
wail *(28)* long cry of grief
devoid *(29)* lacking

E ach night, before they went to bed, the children used to 1
chat together. Seating themselves on the ledge of the
broad oven, they uttered whatever came into their minds.
Through the dim window the evening twilight peered into the
room with dream-laden eyes. Out of every corner the silent
shadows drifted upwards, carrying strange stories with them.

They spoke of whatever came to their minds, but to their 2
minds came only pleasant stories of sunlight and warmth inter-
woven with love and hope. The whole future was one long
bright holiday; no Lent between Christmas and Eastertide. Over
there, somewhere behind the flowered curtain, all life, blinking
and throbbing, silently poured from the light into light. Words
were whispered and only half understood. No story had any
beginning, nor definite form. No story had an end. At times all
four children spoke at once, yet none confused the other. All
gazed enthralled into a beauteous heavenly light where each
word was clear and true, where each story had a clear and living
face, and each tale its glorious finish.

The children bore so marked a resemblance to one another 3
that in the dim twilight the face of the youngest, four-year-old
Tonchek, could not be distinguished from that of the ten-year-

From *Dream Visions* by Ivan Cankar. Translated from Slovenian by Helen P.
Hlacha. "Children and Old Folks" first appeared in English in 1925 in
Great Short Stories of the World, published by The World Publishing Com-
pany, Cleveland–New York.

old Loizka, the eldest. All had thin, narrow faces and large, wide-open eyes—introspective eyes.

That evening, something unknown from an unknown place 4 reached with violent hand into that heavenly light and struck pitilessly among the holidays, the stories, and legends. The post had brought tidings that the father "had fallen" on Italian soil. Something unknown, new, strange, entirely incomprehensible rose before them. It stood there, tall and broad, but had neither face, nor eyes, nor mouth. Nowhere did it belong, not to that clamorous life before the church and on the street, nor to that warm twilight around the oven, nor to the stories.

It was nothing joyful, but neither was it particularly sor- 5 rowful, for it was dead; because it had no eyes that it might by their look reveal wherefore and whence, and no mouth that it might explain by words. Thought stood humbly and timidly before that enormous apparition as before a great black wall, motionless. It approached the wall, and stared dumb and ponderous.

"But when will he come back?" asked Tonchek, wonderingly. 6

Loizka nudged him with an angry look. "How can he come 7 back if he has fallen?"

All lapsed into silence. They stood before that great black 8 wall, and beyond it they could not see.

"I'm going to war, too!" unexpectedly announced seven- 9 year-old Matiche, as if he had swiftly hit up the right thought. That was evidently all that it was necessary to say.

"You're too small," admonished four-year-old Tonchek, in a 10 deep voice. Tonchek still wore dresses!

Milka, the thinnest and sickliest of them, who was wrapped 11 in her mother's large shawl and resembled a wayfarer's pack, asked in her soft little voice from somewhere out of the shadows, "What is war like? Tell us, Matiche, tell us that story!"

Matiche explained, "Well, war is like this. People stab each 12 other with knives, cut each other down with swords, and shoot each other with guns. The more you stab and cut down, the better it is. Nobody says anything to you, 'cause that's how it has to be. That's war."

"But why do they stab and cut each other down?" Milka 13
insisted.

"For the Emperor!" said Matiche, and all were silent. 14

In the dim distance before their clouded eyes appeared 15
something mighty, glistening with the radiance of glory. They
sat motionless, their breaths barely daring to escape their
mouths, as in church at the benediction.

Then Matiche again swiftly gathered his thoughts; possibly 16
just to dispel the silence which lay so heavy over them. "I'm
going to war, too. Against the enemy."

"What is the enemy like? Has he horns?" suddenly inquired 17
the thin voice of Milka.

" 'Course he has, else how could he be the enemy?" seri- 18
ously, almost angrily replied Tonchek in emphatic tones. And
now not even Matiche himself knew the correct answer.

"I don't think he—has them!" he said slowly, haltingly. 19

"How can he have horns? He's a person like us," voiced 20
Loizka unwillingly. Then, reconsidering, she added, "Only he
has no soul."

After a lengthy pause Tonchek inquired, "But how does a 21
person fall in the war? Like this, backward?" And he illustrated
the point.

"They kill him to death!" calmly explained Matiche. 22

"Father promised to bring me a gun." 23

"How can he bring you a gun if he has fallen?" Loizka 24
roughly retorted.

"And they killed him—to death?" 25

"To death." 26

Through the youthful and wide-open eyes silence and sor- 27
row stared into darkness, into something unknown, to heart and
mind inconceivable.

At the same time on a bench before the cottage sat the grand- 28
father and grandmother. The last red rays of the sun glowed
through the dark foliage in the garden. The evening was silent
except for a smothered, prolonged sob, already grown hoarse,
which came from the stable. In all probability it was the wail of
the young mother who had gone there to tend the livestock.

The two old people sat deeply bowed, close to one another, 29 and held each other's hands as they had not done for a long time. They gazed into the heavenly afterglow with eyes devoid of tears, and did not speak.

 Focusing on the Story

1   What piece of news has arrived in the mail? How do the children react to the news?

2   What is Matiche's definition of war? For whom is war fought?

3   What does Tonchek think the enemy looks like? What does the enemy lack according to Loizka?

4   In paragraph 5, the pronoun *it* is used more than half a dozen times. What does *it* refer to?

5   How do the mother and grandparents react to the tragic news?

 Interpreting and Evaluating

1   Despite his grisly description of war, Matiche declares that he's "going to war, too. Against the enemy." Why would he want to go to war?

2   How would you describe the author's attitude to the subject matter (the tone of the story)? What effect does such a tone have on the story as a whole? Explain.

3   The innocent characters and the peaceful setting create a calm and tranquil mood (the feeling the reader is left with), a strange and ironic contrast to the subject matter of war. Is the contrast effective? Explain.

4   Who are the victims of war? Does anyone benefit? If so, who? Explain.

5   The events in the story take place in Slovenia, a republic in the northwestern part of former Yugoslavia, during World War I. This area is also beset with strife today. Why are people constantly fighting in this area? Why do certain regions seem to be more prone or inclined to unrest than others?

Ideas For Writing and Further Discussion

1 What are some causes of armed conflict? Write an essay in which you explore several causes of war.

Suggested *thesis*: three or four such causes.

Each *body paragraph* should explore one cause.

2 Benjamin Franklin wrote that there never was a good war or a bad peace. Do you agree that a disadvantageous peace is better than a just war? Take a stand and write an essay either agreeing or disagreeing with Benjamin Franklin's statement.

Suggested *thesis*: two or three reasons why you agree or disagree with the statement.

Each *body paragraph* should explore one reason. Use facts, statistics, examples, or anecdotes (brief stories) to support your reasons.

Just Lather, That's All

Hernando Téllez

About the Author

Hernando Téllez, born in 1908, is a Colombian politician, diplomat, and author who often writes about political conflicts in South America.

 Something to Think About

How does murdering someone with a knife or a razor at close range differ from executing or killing someone in an armed conflict? Which form of killing might be more difficult?

 Words to Keep in Mind

lather *(title)* foam formed by soap

strop *(1)* thick leather strap used to sharpen razors

fatigue *(9)* exhaustion, tiredness

caress *(9)* gentle touch

feigned *(9)* pretended

faction *(9)* a group working for a common cause against, for example, the government

imposes *(9)* places, sets forth, often by authority or force

emitted *(9)* let out

conscientious *(9)* doing what one knows is right; honest

swirls *(10)* curls

rejuvenated *(11)* made young

ineradicable *(11)* cannot be gotten rid of or removed

avenger *(11)* one who wants to punish justly for something wrong

He said nothing when he entered. I was passing the best   1
of my razors back and forth on a strop. When I recognized him I started to tremble. But he didn't notice. Hoping to
conceal my emotion, I continued sharpening the razor. I tested it
on the meat of my thumb, and then held it up to the light. At that
moment he took off the bullet-studded belt that his gun holster
dangled from. He hung it up on a wall hook and placed his military cap over it. Then he turned to me, loosening the knot of his
tie, and said, "It's hot as hell. Give me a shave." He sat in the
chair.

I estimated he had a four-day beard. The four days taken up   2
by the latest expedition in search of our troops. His face seemed
reddened, burned by the sun. Carefully, I began to prepare the
soap. I cut off a few slices, dropped them into the cup, mixed in a
bit of warm water, and began to stir with the brush. Immediately
the foam began to rise. "The other boys in the group should
have this much beard, too." I continued stirring the lather.

"But we did all right, you know. We got the main ones. We   3
brought back some dead, and we've got some others still alive.
But pretty soon they'll all be dead."

"How many did you catch?" I asked.   4

"Fourteen. We had to go pretty deep into the woods to find   5
them. But we'll get even. Not one of them comes out of this
alive, not one." He leaned back on the chair when he saw me
with the lather-covered brush in my hand. I still had to put the

sheet on him. No doubt about it, I was upset. I took a sheet out of a drawer and knotted it around my customer's neck. He wouldn't stop talking. He probably thought I was in sympathy with his party.

"The town must have learned a lesson from what we did the other day," he said.   6

"Yes," I replied, securing the knot at his dark, sweaty neck.   7

"That was a fine show, eh?"   8

"Very good," I answered, turning back for the brush. The man closed his eyes with a gesture of fatigue and sat waiting for the cool caress of the soap. I had never had him so close to me. The day he ordered the whole town to file into the patio of the school to see the four rebels hanging there, I came face-to-face with him for an instant. But the sight of the mutilated bodies kept me from noticing the face of the man who had directed it all, the face I was now about to take into my hands. It was not an unpleasant face, certainly. And the beard, which made him seem a bit older than he was, didn't suit him badly at all. His name was Torres. Captain Torres. A man of imagination, because who else would have thought of hanging the naked rebels and then holding target practice on certain parts of their bodies? I began to apply the first layer of soap. With his eyes closed, he continued. "Without any effort I could go straight to sleep," he said, "but there's plenty to do this afternoon." I stopped the lathering and asked with a feigned lack of interest: "A firing squad?" "Something like that, but a little slower." I got on with the job of lathering his beard. My hands started trembling again. The man could not possibly realize it, and this was in my favor. But I would have preferred that he hadn't come. It was likely that many of our faction had seen him enter. And an enemy under one's roof imposes certain conditions. I would be obliged to shave that beard like any other one, carefully, gently, like that of any customer, taking pains to see that no single pore emitted a drop of blood. Being careful to see that the little tufts of hair did not lead the blade astray. Seeing that his skin ended up clean, soft, and healthy, so that passing the back of my hand over it I couldn't feel a hair. Yes, I was secretly a rebel, but I was also a conscientious barber, and proud of the preciseness of my profession. And this four days' growth of beard was a fitting challenge.

I took the razor, opened up the two protective arms, exposed 10 the blade and began the job, from one of the sideburns downward. The razor responded beautifully. His beard was inflexible and hard, not too long, but thick. Bit by bit the skin emerged. The razor rasped along, making its customary sound as fluffs of lather mixed with bits of hair gathered along the blade. I paused a moment to clean it, then took up the strop again to sharpen the razor, because I'm a barber who does things properly. The man, who had kept his eyes closed, opened them now, removed one of his hands from under the sheet, felt the spot on his face where the soap had been cleared off, and said, "Come to the school today at six o'clock." "The same thing as the other day?" I asked, horrified. "It could be better," he replied. "'What do you plan to do?" "I don't know yet. But we'll amuse ourselves." Once more he leaned back and closed his eyes. I approached him with the razor poised. "Do you plan to punish them all?" I ventured timidly. "All." The soap was drying on his face. I had to hurry. In the mirror I looked toward the street. It was the same as ever: the grocery store with two or three customers in it. Then I glanced at the clock: two twenty in the afternoon. The razor continued on its downward stroke. Now from the other sideburn down. A thick, blue beard. He should have let it grow like some poets or priests do. It would suit him well. A lot of people wouldn't recognize him. Much to his benefit, I thought, as I attempted to cover the neck area smoothly. There, for sure, the razor had to be handled masterfully, since the hair, although softer, grew into little swirls. A curly beard. One of the tiny pores could be opened up and issue forth its pearl of blood. A good barber such as I prides himself on never allowing this to happen to a client. And this was a first-class client. How many of us had he ordered shot? How many of us had he ordered mutilated? It was better not to think about it. Torres did not know that I was his enemy. He did not know it nor did the rest. It was a secret shared by very few, precisely so that I could inform the revolutionaries of what Torres was doing in the town and of what he was planning each time he undertook a rebel-hunting excursion. So it was going to be very difficult to explain that I had him right in my hands and let him go peacefully—alive and shaved.

The beard was now almost completely gone. He seemed 11 younger, less burdened by years than when he had arrived. I suppose this always happens with men who visit barbershops. Under the stroke of my razor Torres was being rejuvenated— rejuvenated because I am a good barber, the best in the town, if I may say so. A little more lather here, under his chin, on his Adam's apple, on this big vein. How hot it is getting! Torres must be sweating as much as I. But he is not afraid. He is a calm man, who is not even thinking about what he is going to do with the prisoners this afternoon. On the other hand I, with this razor in my hands, stroking and restroking this skin, trying to keep blood from oozing from these pores, can't even think clearly. Damn him for coming, because I'm a revolutionary and not a murderer. And how easy it would be to kill him. And he deserves it. Does he? No! What the devil! No one deserves to have someone else make the sacrifice of becoming a murderer. What do you gain by it? Nothing. Others come along and still others, and the first ones kill the second ones and they the next ones and it goes on like this until everything is a sea of blood. I could cut this throat just so, zip! zip! I wouldn't give him time to complain and since he has his eyes closed he wouldn't see the glistening knife blade or my glistening eyes. But I'm trembling like a real murderer. Out of his neck a gush of blood would spout onto the sheet, on the chair, on my hands, on the floor. I would have to close the door. And the blood would keep inching along the floor, warm, ineradicable, uncontainable, until it reached the street, like a little scarlet stream. I'm sure that one solid stroke, one deep incision, would prevent any pain. He wouldn't suffer. But what would I do with the body? Where would I hide it? I would have to flee, leaving all I have behind, and take refuge far away, far, far away. But they would follow until they found me. "Captain Torres' murderer. He slit his throat while he was shaving him—a coward." And then on the other side. "The avenger of us all. A name to remember. (And here they would mention my name.) He was the town barber. No one knew he was defending our cause."

And what of all this? Murderer or hero? My destiny depends 12 on the edge of this blade. I can turn my hand a bit more, press a little harder on the razor, and sink it in. The skin would give way like silk, like rubber, like the strop. There is nothing more tender than human skin and the blood is always there, ready to pour forth. A blade like this doesn't fail. It is my best. But I don't want to be a murderer, no sir. You came to me for a shave. And I perform my work honorably. . . . I don't want blood on my hands. Just lather, that's all. You are an executioner and I am only a barber. Each person has his own place in the scheme of things. That's right. His own place.

Now his chin had been stroked clean and smooth. The man 13 sat up and looked into the mirror. He rubbed his hands over his skin and felt it fresh, like new.

"Thanks," he said. He went to the hanger for his belt, pistol 14 and cap. I must have been very pale; my shirt felt soaked. Torres finished adjusting the buckle, straightened his pistol in the holster and after automatically smoothing down his hair, he put on the cap. From his pants pocket he took out several coins to pay me for my services. And he began to head toward the door. In the doorway he paused for a moment, and turning to me he said:

"They told me that you'd kill me. I came to find out. But 15 killing isn't easy. You can take my word for it." And he headed on down the street.

 Focusing on the Story

1   Who is Captain Torres, the barber's customer? Who or what does he represent? With which side does the barber sympathize?

2   Where has Captain Torres been for the last four days? What has he been up to during this time?

3   What does Captain Torres plan to do with the captured rebels who are still alive?

4   An internal conflict is a conflict within a character. What is the barber's internal conflict or dilemma?

5   Why does the barber decide not to kill Torres?

 Interpreting and Evaluating

1   The setting (time and place) of the story is a barber shop on a hot day. However, the reader must infer in what country the action occurs. On what continent is the country? What is happening politically in this country?

2   The barber says that his ties to the revolution were kept secret so that he could inform the revolutionaries of what Torres was up to. Why would the barber be a good choice for an informer?

3   If the barber had killed Torres, how might the barber have been considered a cowardly murderer on one hand and a heroic avenger on the other?

4   At the end of the story the reader learns that Captain Torres has been told that the barber would kill him, yet Torres remains completely cool while the barber is trembling and sweating. Is Torres a fool to let the barber get so close to him with a sharp razor? What does Torres know about human behavior?

5   Should the barber be praised or criticized for his action? Should he have killed Captain Torres, who, after all, had killed several of the barber's comrades? Explain.

 An Idea for Writing and Further Discussion

Have you ever been faced with a difficult decision? What was your dilemma? What did you finally decide to do? Write about a time when you were faced with a difficult decision. Describe your dilemma, and explain why you finally chose to make the decision that you made.

It's not necessary to write a formal thesis statement in a narrative essay, but you may wish to start with a general statement that expresses an attitude toward the experience.

Old Man at the Bridge

Ernest Hemingway

About the Author

Ernest Hemingway was born in Indiana in 1899. During World War I, he served as an ambulance driver on the Italian front, and after the war had ended he returned to Europe as a foreign correspondent. In 1954, Hemingway received the Nobel Prize for literature but died only seven years later by suicide.

 Something to Think About

Are violence and war inevitable? Who suffers the most in war? What is the best way for men and women to face physical danger?

 Words to Keep in Mind

spectacles *(1)* eyeglasses

pontoons *(1)* cylinders filled with air to support a temporary bridge

Ebro Delta *(11)* area where the Ebro river flows into the Mediterranean near Barcelona

Fascists *(36)* Spanish troops under General Franco in the Spanish Civil War in 1936

n old man with steel rimmed spectacles and very dusty   1
clothes sat by the side of the road. There was a pontoon

bridge across the river and carts, trucks, and men, women and children were crossing it. The mule-drawn carts staggered up the steep bank from the bridge with soldiers helping push against the spokes of the wheels. The trucks ground up and away heading out of it all and the peasants plodded along in the ankle deep dust. But the old man sat there without moving. He was too tired to go any farther.

It was my business to cross the bridge, explore the bridge- 2 head beyond and find out to what point the enemy had advanced. I did this and returned over the bridge. There were not so many carts now and very few people on foot, but the old man was still there.

"Where do you come from?" I asked him. 3

"From San Carlos," he said, and smiled. 4

That was his native town and so it gave him pleasure to 5 mention it and he smiled.

"I was taking care of animals," he explained. 6

"Oh," I said, not quite understanding. 7

"Yes," he said, "I stayed, you see, taking care of animals. I 8 was the last one to leave the town of San Carlos."

He did not look like a shepherd nor a herdsman and I looked 9 at his black dusty clothes and his gray dusty face and his steel rimmed spectacles and said, "What animals were they?"

"Various animals," he said, and shook his head. "I had to 10 leave them."

I was watching the bridge and the African looking country 11 of the Ebro Delta and wondering how long now it would be before we would see the enemy, and listening all the while for the first noises that would signal that ever mysterious event called contact, and the old man still sat there.

"'What animals were they?" I asked. 12

"There were three animals altogether," he explained. "There 13 were two goats and a cat and then there were four pairs of pigeons."

"And you had to leave them?" I asked. 14

"Yes. Because of the artillery. The captain told me to go 15 because of the artillery."

"And you have no family?" I asked, watching the far end of   16
the bridge where a few last carts were hurrying down the slope
of the bank.

"No" he said, "only the animals I stated. The cat, of course,   17
will be all right. A cat can look out for itself, but I cannot think
what will become of the others."

"What politics have you?" I asked.   18

"I am without politics," he said. "I am seventy-six years old. I have   19
come twelve kilometers now and I think now I can go no further."

"This is not a good place to stop," I said. "If you can make it,   20
there are trucks up the road where it forks for Tortosa."

"I will wait a while,"' he said, "and then I will go. Where do   21
the trucks go?"

"Towards Barcelona," I told him.   22

"I know no one in that direction," he said, "but thank you   23
very much. Thank you again very much."

He looked at me very blankly and tiredly, then said, having   24
to share his worry with some one, "The cat will be all right, I am
sure. There is no need to be unquiet about the cat. But the others.
Now what do you think about the others?"

"Why they'll probably come through it all right."   25

"You think so?"   26

"Why not," I said, watching the far bank where now there   27
were no carts.

"But what will they do under the artillery when I was told to   28
leave because of the artillery?"

"Did you leave the dove cage unlocked?" I asked.   29

"Yes."   30

"Then they'll fly."   31

"Yes, certainly they'll fly. But the others. It's better not to   32
think about the others," he said.

"If you are rested I would go," I urged. "Get up and try to   33
walk now."

"Thank you," he said and got to his feet, swayed from side to   34
side and then sat down backwards in the dust.

"I was taking care of animals," he said dully, but no longer to   35
me. "I was only taking care of animals."

There was nothing to do about him. It was Easter Sunday 36 and the Fascists were advancing toward the Ebro. It was a gray overcast day with a low ceiling so their planes were not up. That and the fact that cats know how to look after themselves was all the good luck that old man would ever have.

Focusing on the Story

1   Why are carts, trucks, men, women, and children crossing the bridge? What's going on?

2   The setting (place and time) of the story is not stated directly but rather implied. In what country and during which time does the story take place?

3   Who is the narrator (the character who tells the story), and what can you say about him? What is his job?

4   Describe the old man. What animals has the old man left behind? Which ones is he most worried about? What's the irony in this situation?

5   How is the old man lucky on the particular day the narrator meets him?

Interpreting and Evaluating

1   Why does the old man smile when he tells the narrator that he is from San Carlos? Why doesn't he want to go to Barcelona? Doesn't he realize the danger he is in?

2   The narrator asks the old man what politics he has. What does this question mean? Would the outcome have changed for the old man if his answer had been different?

3   A symbol is something that has meaning beyond the most obvious literal meaning. For example, a flag is just a piece of cloth but often symbolizes a country or state. What do doves usually symbolize? How may the bridge in this story be considered a symbol, and what may the bridge symbolize?

4   The old man keeps repeating that he was only taking care of his animals. Nevertheless, what will most likely happen to him the next day or in the next few days? Do you feel sorry for the old man? How does the old man face the situation? If you had been in the old man's place, would you have shown more signs of fear?

5   What was Hemingway's opinion of war, judging from this story?

 Ideas for Writing and Further Discussion

1   Write a paragraph or two about a time when you tried to help someone but couldn't. Describe the situation, and explain why the other person refused your help. How did the incident make you feel?

2   Have you ever had to face a dangerous situation head on? How did you feel and how did you react? Write a narrative essay about a dangerous or frightening experience you have had. Describe what happened and how you handled it. How did you feel? What was the outcome? Did you learn anything about your own feelings from the experience?

It's not necessary to write a formal thesis statement in a narrative essay, but you may wish to start with a general statement that expresses your attitude toward the experience.

 An Additional Idea for Discussion and Writing

Think of the message (theme) that the authors of "Children and Old Folks" and "Old Man at the Bridge" convey to the reader. Do innocent people suffer in wars? How do the authors of these two stories convey the message that innocent people suffer in wars?

Write an essay in which you discuss the different techniques that authors Ivan Cankar and Ernest Hemingway use to convey the reality of war. For example, both stories have a similar tone, for both authors editorialize. Hemingway selects only those details that make us feel sorry for the old man: he's old, alone, tired, and confused. He is also heartbroken that he's had to abandon his animals and afraid of leaving the familiar for the unfamiliar. Cankar's technique is similar. What about the characters? How are they both similar and different?

Suggested *thesis*: two or three ways each author tries to convey the message that innocent people suffer in wars.

Each *body paragraph* should explore one way.